Flowers
For a Grieving Mom

Flowers

For a Grieving Mom

100 Day Devotional
for Moms Who Have Lost a Child

ROXANNE EILERS

Dedication

This devotional is dedicated to every dear mom who has lost a child or children. May God bring some encouragement, validation, strength and comfort to you as you ponder each day of this devotional.

Introduction

This devotional is a compilation of especially selected Scriptures, blogs from my group on Face Book, *Flowers for a Grieving Mom*, and prayers from my heart.

I know how it feels to lose a child. I know the pain and finality. I can relate to you in many ways. I pray that this *100 Day Devotional* will speak to your heart in a deep and profound way, ever moving you to keep trusting in a trustworthy God and to keep holding firm to your hope following the light that shines at the end of the tunnel.

From my heart to yours,
Roxanne

Day 1

2 Corinthians 1:8-10 "We do not want you to be uninformed, brothers and sisters, about the troubles we experienced in the province of Asia. We were under great pressure, far beyond our ability to endure, so that we despaired of life itself. Indeed, we felt we had received the sentence of death. But this happened that we might not rely on ourselves but on God, who raises the dead. He has delivered us from such a deadly peril, and he will deliver us again. On him we have set our hope that he will continue to deliver us..."

I'M GLAD I can be honest with you all. I wish I could always be a tower of strength and comfort to you but alas, I am a fragile human being and I am very weak at times. Like today. I had to go to Target to pick up some gifts for a wedding shower. I had mapped out what I was going to do from this Saturday into the first week of February. Then as I sat in the car I felt I couldn't do any of those things. I thought about Joe's date coming up in February when he died—I don't like going through this. I felt completely overwhelmed.

Yesterday I was just talking about pacing ourselves

"

and saying yes and no when we need to in order to protect ourselves emotionally—especially after the trauma of our great loss. Not to overload. Well I was overloaded and I called my sister and told her all my heart trying to fight tears back. We talked and she helped me get my perspective in better shape.

Sometimes I forget just what a tragedy it was to have lost my only son to a car accident. My heart was shattered. As I feel stronger I am tricked into believing that I can move ahead full speed. I am tricked into believing that I am all healed up and so I lose my awareness of my utter vulnerability and fragility. I become a target for becoming overwhelmed.

Moms, this deal of grief is a big thing that has happened to us. We cannot expect to come completely through it any time soon. We can, however, experience more and more levels of healing and acceptance.

Be on guard and remember that the loss of our child is monumental and recovering from the blow of it will take time.

And this is okay.

Dear Father, give my heart grace to face what happened. As I remember the shock of losing my child comfort me and heal my emotions a little more. Give me wisdom to know my limits and my vulnerability. Give me wisdom to know how to take care of myself emotionally during this difficult season of grief. Amen.

Day 2

*2 Timothy 1:12 "That is why I am suf-
fering as I am. Yet this is no cause for shame,
because I know whom I have believed, and
am convinced that he is able to guard what
I have entrusted to him until that day."*

TODAY IS THE two-year anniversary of when Joe went to heaven. He left us February 15, 2016.He moved away to his home in heaven where we will meet him next time.

How do I feel today? I miss him terribly. I am holding confidently to my faith and hope in seeing him again. Our separation is only temporary. I commit him to the wonderful merciful hand of Jesus who loves him more than I could ever—His Creator. I am honored to have been Joe's mom on earth. What a gift! I know he would want me to live fully in this life. So I strive to. I feel our hearts are bonded for all time for he has become such a part of me. God will have to fill that deep longing I have to see him here on earth.

My broken heart is healing. Over these last two years God has brought me so far. Still at times my head spins with all that has happened. I will never forget this date although others will. I will never forget that night when we were told the news of his physical death on earth. I will not live there though—for I cannot change it, nor can I bring my son back to me. One day I will go to him.

I feel sober. I feel a certain reverence for his life he lived here. I honor his memory on this day he graduated and thank God for him.

Dear Father, support my heart today. Wrap Your comforting Holy Spirit around me. As I ponder upon this day and the memories that surround it, fill my heart with continued hope. Help me to honor my child by choosing healing and life. Amen.

Day 3

Isaiah 40:29 "He gives strength to the weary and increases the power of the weak."

Moms, God is faithful to give strength to the weary and to bind up the wounds of the griever. But we first must grieve. As we do He gives us the ability and strength to make it through each episode of pain. I have watched God at work in my own life—comforting, strengthening, restoring, and healing.

I was reminded the other day, when I had to embrace the calendar day my son died, how deep grief can go. This day will come around every year. This year, being my second, more layers of pain and wounds have been revealed and peeled away from my heart.

What did I do? I started to feel overwhelmed. That huge tidal wave was trying to pull me down under but I remembered how to keep myself afloat. I felt the feelings and then invited God to enter into my sorrow and grief with me to heal my wounded soul and emotions. I laid it down at the cross and began to be thankful for the moments I enjoyed the gift of my son. I called one of my grief mentors for more support and she encouraged me with good words—words of hope—which was just what I needed to help me get back into a healthy perspective.

Dear Father, help me to have a healthy perspective during this time of grief. Help me to hold strong to my hope and faith in You. Thank You for Your sure promise to bring me through this valley. Amen.

Day 4

Hebrews 10:23 "Let us hold unswervingly to the hope we profess, for he who promised is faithful."

THERE ARE TIMES when we feel like nothing is working to ease our pain of sorrow. We've prayed, cried, talked, listened, read. We feel alone in our sorrow. One thing I know is that I have felt like this myself. I have felt desperate for some relief for my torn emotions and broken heart.

There are times when we cry out to God and we feel nothing, hear nothing—where is our God when we need Him?

God asks us to believe in Him even if everything tells us different. When doubts are the only thoughts that crowd our minds— God asks us to have faith regardless of what we feel. Feelings have nothing to do with faith. Faith has everything to do with obedience to God and He says not to fear only believe. Our emotions and feelings may

scream like children
in a tantrum. However,
our "will" is like the mother and she says what
will be. So with our will we choose to trust in a God who declares He is always with us and loves us. We choose to place our confidence in the only One who can really help us to live again. I know for sure this is not easy to do especially when we are engulfed and hidden in the darkness of grief.

But God is there. He will never let us down. We can lean on Him and His strength. He will bring us through even if it's moment by moment.

Remember to believe and trust first before you see any results. If you do, God will never let you down. He will come through and hear your cries. Let your faith grow during this hard time.

Dear Father, my heart needs to be reassured that You are with me right now. Let me feel Your presence in a new and fresh way today. Take the faith I do have and please increase it. I do believe that You will calm my emotions and give me peace. Amen.

Day 5

*1 Thessalonians 5:11 "Therefore encourage
one another and build each other up,
just as in fact you are doing."*

I AM LEARNING MORE and more about grief and the journey. I am learning that not everybody wants to hear our story. It offends some. It frightens others—perhaps they fear for their own children and our personal story is too close to home. Sometimes family is tired of hearing about our loss. They feel we should be over it by now. Remember that most people forget the trauma that we experienced and that we are daily reminded of it. They can only take so much because they have their own issues. We cannot expect others to always understand where we are at. And it has to be okay for them to distance themselves if they need to. Then you will find those who will draw near with a heart that is deeply touched and cares.

It is vital for you to tell and retell your story of loss to those who can hear it and validate your feelings. Find safe people (usually in grief groups and close friends, and some family members) who will listen again and again. I surround myself with these kinds of people. Bless my sisters and brothers who hear me and comfort me again and again. They are a gift. Then my close friends who love me—they let me talk and they validate my feelings. And of course those moms who have also experienced this kind of a loss will listen with intent.

I remember a sweet friend who started her grief journey around the time I did. Sometimes we'd meet at Coffee Bean and tell our stories over and over. Thank you, Diane.

It's in telling the story that we begin to accept the truth a little more and get some perspective. We are comforted to know we are not alone in our desperate pain. The world may not know the huge blow that brought your ship down but you will always know and need a friend to share it with.

Thank you to all of you who have listened to my story even though you have heard it so many times. You have helped me to heal.

Dear Father, please bring into my life just the people I need to give me support and to cheer me on in this difficult journey. Give me the courage to share my story with those who want to listen. Lead me to these special people. Please support my heart with love. Amen.

Day 6

2 Corinthians 1:3-4 "Praise be to the God and Father of our Lord Jesus Christ, the Father of compassion and the God of all comfort, who comforts us in all our troubles, so that we can comfort those in any trouble with the comfort we ourselves receive from God."

ALL OF A sudden it's a shock all over again. The reality becomes clearer than you want to see it. How can it be—my boy gone from me? I pass the street where he was hit by that car and can feel the shock grab at my heart—I gasp! What do I do with this horrible reality when it raises its head again?

I know I need to accept the fact of his death and I do, but a part of me doesn't. I think because I don't want to forget him. Again I turn my heart reins over to Jesus and let Him hold me and rock me and soothe me. He knows—He knows.

Dear Father, guard my heart! Hold me together inside. Help me to accept the facts about my child's death. I feel so afraid. Please give me the grace I need each time I am hit by this reality. **Amen.**

Day 7

Psalm 18:2 "The LORD is my rock, my fortress, and my savior; my God is my rock, in whom I find protection. He is my shield, the power that saves me, and my place of safety."

YOU CANNOT PUT grief in an envelope and shove it back in a drawer somewhere. No. You cannot ignore grief and put it off for later because you're tired of it. Oh you can stuff it deep down inside your heart and try to numb it, but sooner or later it will surface and be more persistent than ever. Grief demands our attention—it demands to be acknowledged, felt and dealt with. We have to go through it. Go through it, however long it may take.

I've tried to hurry grief but it won't be hurried. So I'm letting it have its way. I'm learning to ride the waves even if they take me way out to a place

I've never been before. I am daily learning that God is with me in all my places of grief and His hand is gently leading me to the places where I can be comforted, rested, encouraged and restored. I will trust in Him for He is my Rock of Safety.

Dear Father, please give me the courage to face my feelings of grief when they come. Help me to look into Your eyes and see and feel Your renewing strength. Place Your hands under my arms and lift me up to where all I can see is Your glory and beauty. When that wave comes to take me out further than I ever wanted to go, help me to flow with it. To swim instead of sink. Help me to trust that You will always bring me back to a safe place in You. Amen.

Day 8

*2 Corinthians 5:7 "For we walk
by faith, not by sight."*

THIS WHOLE JOURNEY we walk is really a walk by faith. We cannot see the many things we wish we could. But we have an assurance that God has given us. He never left us without a manual which is our compass in this life. This manual is the Bible. This is the chief way that God communicates with us. He never intended us to be running around lost and scared. He gives us the main crucial answers to life and death. So we put our trust in what He says. We lean upon it and into it to support us. It will if we let it. It is a walk of faith—always a walk of faith, for faith pleases God.

When our child dies it takes active faith to believe that they are in a place called heaven and are at peace in God's presence— flourishing and happy. It takes real faith to believe

that we will indeed
be reunited with them
again. Again it takes persistent faith to walk
and come through our grief—we trust there is a God
there to uphold us. And there is because He tells us
He is. He says, "I will never leave you nor forsake
you. I will not fail you" (Hebrews 13:5).

Dear Father, please strengthen my faith in You and in Your promises. I confess I will and do believe that my child is safe with You and that I will see him/her again. I choose to trust You and what You say in Your Word. I praise You my Father, for You are good to me. I place my complete faith in You. Amen.

Day 9

Jeremiah 29:11 "For I know the thoughts that I think toward you, saith the LORD, thoughts of peace, and not of evil, to give you an expected end" (KJV).

SHOW ME MY purpose Lord, I pray.

I *was* a mom. I'm told once you are a mom you are forever. But now I have no child to mother. Who am I now? I guess I can still call myself a mother, but my role has changed. I'm not fitting in anywhere lately. I'm so tired of not feeling secure in who I am. I know I'm God's beloved daughter, but who am I as me? My likes, dislikes, my longings, dreams and desires?

I am changing. I'll always belong to my heavenly Father, but my purpose isn't clear anymore. It has been greatly clouded. Oh, I can do a lot of things but is that who I am—what I do? What is God teaching me about myself? Where is He leading me? Things are different. I am different. This whole process of grief, healing and growing takes so impatiently long.

I remember I was told to take one baby step at a time. Live one moment at a time. I can do that. Do the next thing that's looking me in the face. God knows where He's taking me.

Day 10

Proverbs 4:18 "The way of the righteous is like the first gleam of dawn, which shines ever brighter until the full light of day" (NLT).

How I loved Joseph and still do. He was the joy of my heart. We were at times inseparable. A love affair with this incredible child. Remembering is of highest importance for us who have lost our little love. (They are always our babies and little loves no matter how old they are.)

I am slowly letting go of the tragic memories—the very painful remembering of my son's deep pain and continual suffering of bipolar mental illness.

The anguish that daily crushed my heart until the announcement of his sudden death. My mind was stuck there for a long while. I thought I would go crazy with grief.

Again, slowly as I'm working through my feelings and stages of grief, as I cling to my God for strength and comfort and to the beautiful people that were divinely placed in my life for such a time as this, I am seeing the light ahead of me. At first it was very, very dim but now it is beginning to glow brighter as I choose not to live in sadness forever but daily take baby steps to healing. I must choose.

Dear Father, Thank You so much for giving me a beautiful son to love and raise. Continually guide my thoughts to what will build me up and not grieve my soul. Give me visions and dreams of my child as happy and carefree. Secure and stabilize my steps as I continue to live for You in this world. Help me to experience more moments of joy than sorrow. Amen.

Day 11

Psalm 18:28 "You, Lord keep my lamp burning, my God turns my darkness into light (NIV)."

I FELT JOY TODAY! A part of me wanted to fight it—so used to feeling sad. It made me happy to help lift someone's day with a happy word, to have a Coffee Bean drink and go for a walk with a slight warm/cool breeze blowing across my skin. The flowering trees looked a little brighter. I felt lighter.

I think I'm learning not to fear so much of losing this lightness of heart and falling back down the pit of sorrow. I'm learning that this grief thing is a real journey of the heart that takes you up a hill and down into a valley, around a bend and through many detours along the way—detours where you try to find a short cut through, but you always find yourself back on the path again.

I will say that I will continue to learn to lean into my grief, no matter how deep it

gets, and into my
joys, no matter how small
they may be at first.

Dear Father, thank You for joy! Help me to allow my fragile heart to receive that joy fully. Restore unto me the joy of my salvation in You. Help me to find my lasting joy in Your presence and sweetness. Take away the clouds of darkness that constantly threaten to block the sun from its warmth and shine. Thank You again for Your joy!! *Amen.*

Day 12

*Numbers 23:19 "God is no mere human!
He doesn't tell lies or change his mind. God
always keeps his promises" (CVE).*

HOW BROKEN CAN I get? The questions rush into my mind. How will I live without him? How will I ever feel happy again? So many mixed emotions. You know. Anger, because my boy was taken from me. Fear, of facing my future without ever seeing him again. Sadness, because he's not here and I miss him with all my heart. Lost, unsure of myself, who I am now and where I'm going.

Everything changes—I am changing. I tell myself that my God is my surety. He's my Rock. He's unmovable throughout the ages. He never changes and He has a purpose and a plan for all this grief and madness. He says He has a purpose and a plan in the Bible. I lean against His breast and look up into His eyes like a little child and ask, "Show me a glimpse of Your plan and purpose. Give me a glimpse of steady hope."

And you know, He will. I believe Him. He is my hope.

Dear Father, open my spiritual eyes to behold Your person more clearly. Again steady my screaming emotions and thoughts. I am afraid to be without my child. Reassure me that You are near me right now. I cling to You and look to You for my life and breath. Teach me how to live again, my Father. Amen.

Day 13

Philippians 4:8 "Finally, brothers and sisters, keep your thoughts on whatever is right or deserves praise: things that are true, honorable, fair, pure, acceptable, or commendable" (God's Word Translation).

WHY COULDN'T I have been there? When my son was hit by that car and lying in the dark on the side street all alone. I know he wasn't really alone because God is always with us, but I wasn't there to hold him and comfort him. I wasn't there to kiss him and hold his hand telling him how much I loved him. I wasn't allowed to be there—God knew. It probably would have been too traumatic for me. A homeless man was there. He found my son. I later spoke to him. He told me he held Joe's hand while he lay in the dark until the ambulance came. Joe was already gone when the ambulance got there. He stepped on over to the other side with Jesus.

But there was no closure for me. I just kept replaying what that scene must have looked like that night. I wish I could have been there.

Sometimes we aren't there when our child passes. We feel we have not had proper closure—no real good-byes. Then sometimes we do find our child after they have died and we feel traumatized. Or we are there to hold their hand just before they leave this earth—still, in all we are traumatized. We keep replaying those last weeks, days and moments.

I believe that God wants to heal our traumatized wounded soul. He wants to restore us and heal our memory of how it was. Not that we will ever forget but the memory will not hold that terrible pain every time we think of it.

God is doing just that for me. As I walked to the place where my son was supposed to have been lying on the road, around the corner from where we live, the memory didn't jab me like it did in the beginning. It is losing its power over my heart. I believe it is because I am asking God to heal those memories. He wants to heal your wounds also. Reach out to Him and pour your heart out to Him. Lay those terrible, frightful, hopeless, painful memories at His cross. He will redeem them.

Dear Father, I do lay any terrible, frightful, hopeless and painful memories of the last days of my child's life at the foot of Your cross. Heal the horror, heal the sadness, the anguish, heal the searing pain. Give me a good image to rest my thoughts on. Like, how You were there with my child and You never left their side. Give me rest in my spirit from the guilt and endless wishing that I had been there for their last breath. Lord, please comfort me. Amen.

Day 14

*Job 12:10 "In his hand is the life of every crea-
ture and the breath of all mankind."*

I CAN'T THANK GOD enough for giving me the privilege of being a mother. I was 39 years old when
I had my son. It seems I waited all my life for a
child of my own. My darling baby boy.

Joe filled my life with such joy and then at times
with sorrow but he was the heavenly gift that God
allowed me to bring into this world. My life is different because I had him. My life is different because
I lost him. My life is being transformed because he
lived. My life is richer, deeper, and fuller because of
the love between me and my son. My life is becoming
expectant—I am looking anxiously to the day I find
him in heaven. Even though it has been a huge loss for
me when my son left, I am comforted that God has
brought him safely into his rightful home in heaven.

I am glad Joe lived. I love him so much. I am
relieved that he is safe and deeply loved where he is.
Just imagine we will have fun being together, enjoying
each other's company, telling stories about our lives
on earth in the next life.

Aren't you glad you were given the joy and blessing

of being a mom? Cherish the love of your child that you hold in your heart right now because it is there where love never dies. God, who is pure awesome love Himself, holds you and your child. Always turn to Him and believe Him for He holds the words of life and happiness.

Dear Father, praise You for Your great love You have for me and my child. Thank You for choosing me to be his/her mother. Thank You in advance that I will have my child with me forever one day. Thank You for keeping her/him safe with You in heaven—his/her home. Beautiful Father, thank You for letting me love so deeply and purely. Amen.

Day 15

Psalm 30:5 "…*weeping may endure for a night, but joy cometh in the morning.*"

AND THERE ARE those times when we can't stop sobbing. Tears won't stop. A memory—an ache. A memory—a longing for our child.

I say keep crying those tears. One day you will feel better and find that you are not crying as often or as long.

I remember asking my grief mentor how long I would be crying like this? It frightened me that every day I would be sad and weeping. She said you will find that it will ease up one day.

And she was right. The first year and a half I cried almost every day and then I noticed I would make it a few days without the pouring rain.

Please don't be discouraged if you find yourself in tears again. They are good. Tears are healing. That's how God designed it. These very hard days will also pass as you gently work through your grief and live in the present. Love you.

Dear Father, hold me close to You right now. Put my tears into the beautiful bottle where You carry our tears. Oh, Father give me grace to live for today. Rock me in Your comforting arms and sooth my breaking heart. Hold me close. Amen.

Day 16

Psalm 34:18 "The LORD is close to the broken-hearted and saves those who are crushed in spirit."

Prayer for a Broken Heart

Dear Father, my heart is aching so badly right now. I feel it's broken in millions of pieces. I feel so tired and weak from trying to be strong. The pain goes so deep, Lord—like the depths of the ocean where it seems there is no end. Please give me help. Lift up my heart and repair the pieces and heal me, O God. Hold me up and comfort me with Your love. Infuse hope into my soul so I won't faint all together—but so I can live again. Bring me safely through this dark valley of the shadow of death and let me walk in the land of the living once again. Thank You, Lord for promising to help and heal me. I wait for You to work. In Jesus Name, Amen.

Day 17

Psalm 73:26 "My health may fail, and my spirit may grow weak, but God remains the strength of my heart; he is mine forever" (NLT).

SOMEHOW I AM moving forward and learning to live without my son. I know he is with me in memory and in his love—for love never fails or dies. Love is stronger than death.

In the beginning of my grief journey I had no idea how I would be able to do this—live without him. But I prayed, "Oh God, show me how to live without my son." And He is. You may ask me, how?

I am finding that it is only a moment by moment experience in which God gives strength and perspective. I am shifting my focus to the purposes that I have here on this earth and away from my desire to have Joe with me. I know he will never be able to physically be with me here in this world. I am accepting the fact that he is gone and not coming back here. I am believing and putting my faith to work.

God has given each one of us a measure of faith, so it is important to put it to work—use it and it will grow. I am believing and trusting in a God who says He does not, cannot lie. He says I will see my son again and so I will. Meanwhile I know Joe is safe and in the hands of the One who loves him so very dearly. I also choose daily not to stay in sadness but to cultivate a thankful and praising heart towards God.

If you are at the beginning of your grief journey please take heart and know, as you faithfully work through your feelings and draw near to God moment by moment and ask Him to show you how to live without your child, you will indeed rise up out of the ashes into praise. But don't rush grief—let it have its time. You will know when you want to move on ahead.

Dear Father, please show me how to use the faith You have given me. Help me to believe what I can't see. Give me the grace I need to live in the moment and not to borrow sorrow from tomorrow. Give me strength to cultivate a habit and heart of gratefulness and thanksgiving. Pull me out of any slump that is holding me back from living and assure me of Your healing presence. Amen.

Day 18

THIS LOSS OF ours is a new chapter in our lives as moms. Death is not the end of all. Death is not the end of our child. Death is not the end of us. Our child lives on they're just at a different address than we are. And then, we live on at the old address.

What would you name your new chapter? I think I could name mine, "The Cocoon and the Butterfly" or how about, "The Green Road" for growth.

Can we see there is yet more life to live? More people to love? More lessons in how to live and give?

We will never forget our child. We bring them with us everywhere we go. They are with us through their love and memories. Remember love never dies it just grows stronger. Can we pick up some of the pieces of our lives and take a few more steps into our new world—our new chapter? It's not the end. It is just a new beginning for something new and fresh to emerge from out of the darkness into the light.

Each step we take, God's Word is a Lamp unto our feet and a light unto our path.

Dear Father, please help me to be more accepting of this new chapter in my life. I don't like it. Help me not to fight it but to flow with it. Put courage in my heart and strength in my steps to keep walking towards life again. Take away my fearfulness and ease my anxious heart. I hold to Your hand and know that You are walking with me in this new chapter of my life—You will show me the way. Amen.

Day 19

Isaiah 40:29-31 "He gives strength to the weary and increases the power of the weak. Even youths grow tired and weary, and young men stumble and fall; but those who hope in the LORD will renew their strength. They will soar on wings like eagles; they will run and not grow weary, they will walk and not be faint."

As A MOTHER who has lost a child we never asked or chose this for our life and so we are really forced now to live without them. We have to do something we don't want to do—it goes against all that we are and ever believed about being a mom. We find that we are forced to change, forced to accept what we don't want to, forced to nurse a broken heart, forced to make some new friends—forced to grow or we can choose to lie down and give up which will only hurt ourselves and others. So we pull ourselves up again and again

because no matter
how hard it gets there is
still a higher gain to look forward to which is
a good life to yet live, our precious family and friends,
and the anticipation of seeing our child again.

No matter how hard it gets we will make it through because we have to—giving up is never an option. We have all the strength we need in Christ. So let us keep on getting up and choosing life over and over again.

Dear Father, I want to walk and not faint. I want to run and not grow weary. I confess I cannot live this grief life by myself. It is a maze of unknown places. I need You, Father, to help me accept where I am right now and to accept my lot in this life even though I don't like it at all. I lay my will down upon Your altar of mercy and grace. Not my will, but Yours be done in me. Let Your life arise up in me. Amen.

Day 20

1 Corinthians 13:13 "And now these three remain: faith, hope and love. But the greatest of these is love."

A MOTHER HAS A special relationship with her children—a bond that can never ever be broken. I find it simply amazing how those little ones burrow deep into our hearts and remain there forever even when they are all grown up. God made it that way. Mothers have to endure much in raising their precious child—selflessness is one the biggest things we learn.

Sometimes I just wish I could do it all again. I was so in love with my little son. Every day he grew deeper and deeper into my soul. Now he is a beautiful young man full of youthful life spending his days in the wonderful place where I plan to meet him one day. He will show me all the ropes and places to visit. Every day my love for him continues to grow—it will never ever fade.

We, as mothers, have a different relationship with our child now that we are separated for this short time. This is a time for us to grow and fully blossom in who we are and what we have to give to others. It also gives our child his/her own freedom to spread their wings and get accustomed to their new surroundings in heaven.

We relate to and think of them in a different way now but our special bond is true, unchanging and ever strong.

Dear Father, thank You for my own unique and wonderfully made child! Thank You for the place inside my heart where they have burrowed their way deep with the imprint of their love and person residing there. Thank You, Father, for giving me the privilege of experiencing motherhood even for a period of time. I rejoice in the love that I have for my child and that he/she has for me! Amen.

Day 21

*Proverbs 4:23 "Watch over your heart with all dili-
gence, for from it flow the springs of life" (NASB).*

WE MAY KNOW about the process of grieving
and what we should do in order to heal.
We may know it all in our intellect but it
takes a while before it reaches our hearts.

Today I went for a walk and the weather was so
beautiful. As I was walking back home I saw some
boys playing. Then I passed a house
with some boys out in front
washing the car. Their little
dog ran out to me barking.
I played with him and the
older boy called him back
and told me he was sorry.

We never know when
it's going to hit. Every
boy, every teenager, every
young adult reminds me of
my son. I see him in the eyes
of the young.

As I turned the corner to get
home I began to fight back tears. All

I had were my memories. I wanted Joe. I went into my house and began to really sob. At the same time I was telling myself I knew this would happen and not to be surprised. I was told I would have these moments again and again. Some of what I had learned was finally getting down into my heart. I didn't go down that rabbit hole of darkness and I didn't stay in my sorrow a long time.

Please be patient with yourself especially when you fall into grief more often than you expected. Learn what you can and know that it will take time to go from intellect to heart.

Dear Father, please help me to grasp the lessons of the grief journey I am walking. Help me to be a good student and to allow myself to grow bigger in my soul rather than shrink smaller because of the pain and fear. Father, bless the memories of my child even when they hit hard. Give me the strength to experience them once again and to practice gratitude and thanksgiving. Amen.

Day 22

Psalm 139:13-14 "For you created my inmost being; you knit me together in my mother's womb. I praise you because I am fearfully and wonderfully made; your works are wonderful, I know that full well."

My Grief Journal—Joseph—6/5/93—2/15/16

MAY 8, 2016

I loved being your mother, Joseph. I felt overwhelmed at first when I brought you home. You were this little tiny human being assigned to your dad and I. Gradually I grew more confident. You were quite a handful!

Joseph you meant everything to me. My life was always focused on you just like a mother hen is with her chicks. How great and awesome a gift you were to us even in your hardest days of struggle with bipolar.

I wanted only the best for you and strove daily to bring it to you and your life. I made sure you were taught about the Lord Jesus and His sacrifice for you on the cross. You asked Him into your little heart at the tender age of three and a half. I'm glad you had your faith to help you through those painful days and nights when you were older.

I am so proud of you Son. You fought the good fight of faith and though you stumbled and fell many times, as we all do, you kept asking for God's help. I love you Joseph David.

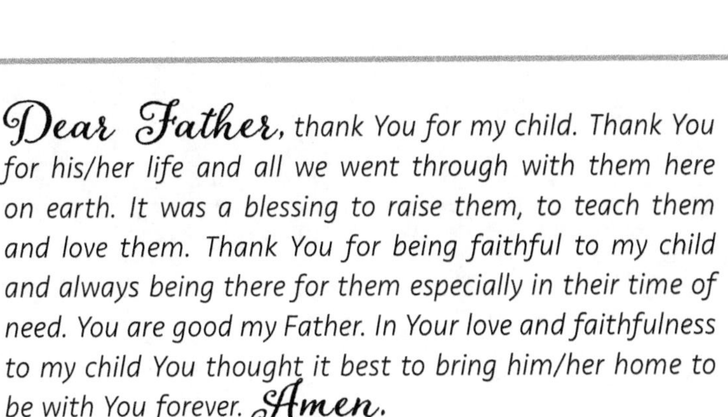

Dear Father, thank You for my child. Thank You for his/her life and all we went through with them here on earth. It was a blessing to raise them, to teach them and love them. Thank You for being faithful to my child and always being there for them especially in their time of need. You are good my Father. In Your love and faithfulness to my child You thought it best to bring him/her home to be with You forever. Amen.

Day 23

IT'S IN THE late afternoon that I begin to feel it—the missing, the emptiness, the loneliness. I try to distract myself from feeling when I am out in public. I don't want anyone to see my tears or broken heart. It's so private, yet shows itself so publicly. The insides show on the outside sooner or later.

I was taking my afternoon walk the other day and I began to remember—the ache came, the missing and then the welling up of the tears. I thought to myself.

No. *I can't. Not here.* I quickly flicked the escaping tears off my cheeks. *Wait,* I told myself, *until you are safely home and then you can remember and miss and feel in peace without scrutinizing eyes searching you.* Then I opened my front door and it all flooded out—oh wretched loss—wretched loss. I was angry and sad. I cried and sobbed and rocked back and forth on his empty bed.

Jesus was with me, He saw, He felt and He knew. I asked Him to hold me. He promised to restore me and comfort me on every side. I chose again to believe that one day this mourning will be turned into dancing.

Dear Father, develop in me a patient heart today. I want to be rid of this pain of grief and yet I find myself going through it again and again. Please pour Your strength inside my soul and stabilize my emotions. Again hold my heart near to You and bring me a little closer to finding my mourning turning into dancing. *Amen.*

Day 24

Psalm 23:1-4 "The Lord is my shepherd; I shall not want. He maketh me to lie down in green pastures: he leadeth me beside the still waters. He restoreth my soul: he leadeth me in the paths of righteousness for his name's sake. Yea, though I walk through the valley of the shadow of death, I will fear no evil: for thou art with me; thy rod and thy staff they comfort me."

As I look back on the hardest days of my grief journey I remember two things that helped me get through. My faith in God played a huge part in my stability of mind, and then the Bible. The words of the Bible are not just ordinary words of a man, but we are told in the book itself that the words were written by men who were completely moved by the Holy Spirit of God. They didn't put their own thoughts down. They recorded just what God told them to. Jesus said the words He spoke to us are spirit and they are life. So when we read the Bible we can draw true strength from what it says. There is so much comfort in its pages. I encourage you to read and let your weary mind ponder and rest upon the words in Psalm 23. Record the promises you find in there.

I can tell you two promises that stand out to me. First, it says "He restores my soul." That means God will heal me emotionally and bring my tumultuous heart into peace. It means He will support me so I don't go crazy with sorrow. It means He will bring me to a place of stability.

The second is "Even though I walk through the valley of the shadow of death, I will fear no evil for you are with me." This means that as I take one step at a time through my grief journey, Jesus is with me, my Good Shepherd. It means my heart does not need to feel overwhelmed because I have the promise here that God will bring me safely through as I lean on Him.

This is good news.

Dear Father, calm my soul when it feels over-whelmed with panic because of my loss. You said I didn't need to fear anything evil because You walk right beside me supporting my fragile heart with Your love. Please continue to restore my brokenness and cover me with Your gentle peace. Amen.

Day 25

1 Thessalonians 4:13-14 "And now, dear brothers and sisters, we want you to know what will happen to the believers who have died so you will not grieve like people who have no hope. For since we believe that Jesus died and was raised to life again, we also believe that when Jesus returns, God will bring back with him the believers who have died" (NLT).

JUST TO HAVE them back for just a little while. To touch them and hug them and kiss them. To look into their eyes and tell them how much they are loved. Just to see them one more time. Our hearts yearn just one more time—that will satisfy. But in reality it never would. We would never want to let them go. But we are not alone— our child is near and can sometimes hear us when we speak.

Sometimes I think God calls them over to Himself in heaven. They sit on His lap and He talks to them all about us and how much we love and miss them. How they love us too!

Don't we love our children so desperately, so completely? God knows we have a bruised heart—a broken crying heart and He promises to heal it if we come to Him and ask Him.

Just to have Joe back for a day. God understands. He will bring us back together at that appointed day!

Day 26

*John 14:1-3 ""Do not let your heart be troubled;
believe in God, believe also in Me. In My Father's
house are many dwelling places; if it were not
so, I would have told you; for I go to prepare a
place for you. If I go and prepare a place for you,
I will come again and receive you to Myself, that
where I am, there you may be also" (NASB).*

WHEN OUR CHILD dies we are forced to look at ourselves, our life, our beliefs about life, how we see others, death and God. We think about the next life. If we aren't sure there is one we begin to search out for answers. We want to have some comfort that we will see our child again. We have to see them again. We search the skies above and wonder if there is a God who cares? Is He real? Is there really a heaven? Or hell? Is Jesus who He said He was? Is the Bible true? Can I trust God to bring me through this deep dark pit? Will His promises stand? Is our child happy? What is he/she doing?

We are forced to make a decision on whether we will believe what Jesus said, that He is the Resurrection and the Life. He who believes in Him will never die spiritually. In His house are many mansions and He went to prepare one for each of us. Will we take that step in the dark and choose to believe there is someone bigger than us who loves us and has revealed Himself to us through the Bible? Will we trust our child to the hand of a loving and good God?

I say we can trust—we can believe—we can make it through our shadowed valley. We can have peace in trusting our child to God. The Judge of all the earth will always do what is right and just. Mercy always triumphs over judgment.

I say we can live our lives with purpose and look forward to a life beyond—a life through faith in the living God—Jesus Christ Himself.

Dear Father, please increase my faith in You and Your Word to me. Help me to understand spiritual things—spiritual words of encouragement that You speak in the Bible. Help me to live in Your words and completely rely on Your unfailing love for me and my child. Open my spiritual eyes to see the truth more clearly as I seek Your face. Amen.

Day 27

Isaiah 40:4 "Every valley shall be raised up, every mountain and hill made low; the rough ground shall become level, the rugged places a plain."

I WAS WARNED IN my grief group not to stay stuck in one of the stages of grief that was not healthy for me—like denial, anger, what if's, sadness. I understand as grievers we can go back and forth in the different stages of grief, but when we stop and park our car in one of these for a period that is too long we can begin to get physically and mentally ill. Our child would not want this ever for us, their precious mom.

It is vital to go through our grief stages and to feel our feelings and work through them. Every one grieves differently so we cannot compare our timeline with another's.

I think the cues our soul gives to us telling us we are spending too much time in one of the stages must be listened to. One of these cues can be that we grow tired of our grief and sorrow, and we are having some thoughts that we would like to move on. Perhaps we are afraid to because we feel we might be betraying our child's memory and think we ought to stay in a mourning state. This is untrue. It is true however, that we can stay in our grief for years and years—that is if we don't work through it or if we push it down and try to ignore it.

I believe it would please our child very much if we embraced life and lived again with happiness as best we can.

Does this mean we love our child less? Absolutely not! We will always carry them in our heart. Sadness, anger, and what if's can still come into our lives at times, but not to the point of being controlled by them and living out of a dark and sad rabbit hole.

Another cue is the warning that we are not getting any better in our pain and we are concerned about it. Sometimes we feel we are regressing way too much. We must get help if we are stuck—help from the many groups and services available for grieving moms. We must learn tools on how to handle our emotions and thoughts—tools on how to have a healthy perspective of our loss. Grief has to be worked through and these groups can help us. Please listen to your cues and take care of yourself. However give yourself enough time to grieve your loss.

There is hope for the future—always hope.

Dear Father, help me not to get stuck in the stages of grief that can be destructive to my emotional well-being. When I feel like I cannot change the stage I am in, and I am sinking, open my eyes and throw me a lifesaver. Inject hope into every fiber of my being. Give me wisdom to know when I am not progressing in my grief journey. Bring me the things I need in order to keep me moving forward step by step. Bring me the assigned people that I need to help me through the seasons of shock, anger, what if's and sadness. Please give me the desire to move gradually into acceptance of my lot. Amen.

Day 28

Psalm 148:1-4 "Praise the Lord.
Praise the Lord from the heavens;
praise him in the heights above.
Praise him, all his angels;
praise him, all his heavenly hosts.
Praise him, sun and moon;
praise him, all you shining stars.
Praise him, you highest heavens
and you waters above the skies."

IN THE MIDST of your sorrow and grief try to find the little things in life that can cheer your weary soul. There is beauty all around you just waiting for you to look and say, "Ah, God, you are an incredible Creator! Your works are awesome!" Every day, just like taking a multi-vitamin, take a few minutes to look around you and take in the good stuff and then be thankful for what you do have and have had.

Dear Father, direct my heart to praise Your name. Direct my thoughts to give You thanks. I choose to rejoice today for all You have given me in my daily life. Shelter, food, protection, health, guidance, sight, hearing, legs to walk, hands to work with. Father I praise and adore You for who You are and for what You have done in my life and for what You will do. *Amen.*

Day 29

Hebrews 12:1 "Therefore, since we are sur-rounded by such a great cloud of witnesses, let us throw off everything that hinders and the sin that so easily entangles. And let us run with per-severance the race marked out for us..."

SOMETIMES ALL WE can do is say nothing but hold out our heart before God. Healing of the heart can only be done by God—it's not a human thing. It is a spiritual thing. We are so limited and without strength at times.

I hold my heart up before my God and the deep ache that it carries. Missing a child who is gone from you is so unspeakably difficult.

Today I felt that ache—my son, I haven't heard your voice for such a long time...such a long time.

One thing I believe is that when we have a child in heaven, he/she is watching over us and leaning forward on heaven's balcony loving us and cheering for us to go on in the fight of our faith. He/

she wants us to know that they still love us and are keeping track of our lives on earth. They can't wait till the day they can run up and put their arms around our necks.

We are told in the Bible that we have a great cloud of witnesses who are cheering us on—these witnesses include our child in heaven who loves us.

Dear Father, give me a glimpse of my child cheering me on from heaven's balcony. Help me to be strong to continue to run the race set before me. Give me an eternal perspective on my child's death. I know that the life to come is real—give me glimpses of this life through my spiritual eyes. Amen.

Day 30

Philippians 3:13-14 "But one thing I do: Forgetting what is behind and straining toward what is ahead, I press on toward the goal to win the prize for which God has called me heavenward in Christ Jesus."

WHAT DOES LETTING go of our grief really mean? It doesn't mean forgetting our child or letting go of our precious memories of them. It does mean, however, that we feel ready to develop a new relationship with them in the sense of how we perceive them now and how we think about them in their new surroundings. We have a different relationship with them now since they've left. They are still the same person and we also but we see them in the light of their new life. See them whole and at peace. We are no longer living in the past with them or even in the present but looking forward to them in the future reunion in Heaven. They have settled into their new surroundings—their new home. They are about the Father's business. They are growing and learning and also anticipating our homecoming. They are no longer that person who was trapped in a fragile human body. They are a spiritual body. They want nothing but joy for us. Can we switch our thinking to perceive them this way?

One thing that never changes is our love for them and their love for us—this remains the same forever. It is as real as it always was even if they are not physically with us. Can we lean into their love for us at the times we feel lonely and sad?

I love this quote from Tabitha Jayne from her article "What 'Letting Go' of Loss Really Means" taken from "The Grief Tool Box." She says that "The love we feel for our loved one remains unchanged after death. If anything it can deepen as we realize truly what our loved one meant to us. By leaning into this love we can let go of grief and create a new connection to our loved one."

I am learning that letting go means to do all these things plus releasing my son into the Hands of Jesus—trusting Him with his death and his life. He is safe. I don't need to cling to my pain for fear of leaving my Joe behind. I can look ahead to see him.

Dear Father, thank You for the hope of seeing my child again. Thank You! Thank You! Death is not the end. Thank You that life and love continue on. Open my eyes of faith to grasp a little more that my child is flourishing in the realms of heaven with You. Thank You that I am surrounded with their love always. Amen.

Day 31

Romans 8:28 "And we know that in all things God works for the good of those who love him, who have been called according to his purpose."

AFTER WE EXPERIENCE a monumental loss like we have our lives are drastically changed. I know mine has been. From the moment I heard the news that my son was gone my life changed. It was messed up, confused, clouded. I felt like I didn't know who I was or what my purpose was in life. For the last 22 years I had been "Joe's mother." Now who was I? I felt misplaced—like I didn't belong anywhere. In my turmoil and confusion I could only sit and watch television and think and pray. "Oh God please show me the way through this deep dark fog. What is my purpose now?"

I was angry, shocked and resistant to this "thing" that barged into my familiar, routine of life. I felt I was missing something. I felt lost because a huge part of me was gone. My world was shaken to the core. All that I ever believed about life, God, the world, death, myself was to be severely tested. What did I really believe? I was exhausted emotionally and physically and I wanted everything back to the way it was.

How could this happen to me? These things happen to others—not me. Not my child. But it happened and I was left to walk the road of grief.

Over the last two years things have changed for me. I am a different person in many ways. It's like I grew up overnight in areas of my life I didn't even know I needed to grow in. Jesus has been my anchor that has held me together. I don't feel so lost—I am finding my niche again. I am beginning to love life again. I am so much happier with who I am and who I am becoming. I am finding my place. Remember this isn't instantaneous.

I love all of the beautiful people that have helped me and do help me on my grief journey. They have paved the way for me by their own aching agony of grief. Now I want to pave the way for others who are just beginning to step onto this unwanted path.

I will say, "You will find your way. You will grow and your faith will become your foundation. You will learn to love deeper and greater than before. You will come to know yourself a little better. And at the right time you will come to accept your lot and move on carrying your child's love and memories in your heart. But for now you must allow yourself to grieve with all your heart for you loved them so very deeply."

Dear Father, I place my hope in You. You are the anchor of my soul where I can run to in times of trouble. Please continue to hold my emotional life stable so I will not live in a state of panic and fear. Soothe my aching heart and help me to build stronger faith in You on this journey. Amen.

Day 32

Romans 11:33-36 "Oh, how great are God's riches and wisdom and knowledge! How impossible it is for us to understand his decisions and his ways! For who can know the LORD's thoughts? Who knows enough to give him advice? And who has given him so much that he needs to pay it back? For everything comes from him and exists by his power and is intended for his glory. All glory to him forever! Amen" (NLT).

LATE LAST NIGHT I pulled out some of the papers that Joe kept in his drawers. They told me of his great battles with drugs and alcohol—his struggles to do good and to do right. They told me about his utter weaknesses and developing strengths. They told me that the most admired person he looked up to was his dad. He placed his spirituality high on his list of important values in his life. How he fought to keep on the healthy track of life. His daily battling with bipolar mental illness wore him out—he tried to make the most of what good days he had. I again realized that only God knew the depths of my son's heart and soul and what he had to face every day. God heard his cries.

I don't like it that he was taken so soon in life. I

don't understand why it couldn't have all
turned out better. I surely don't understand why he had to suffer so. But
God knows. And I am learning that
it is enough to know that God knows
and always held Joe in the palm of
His hand. He says that "all souls are
His" so Joe belonged to Him.

I do know that my dear son is safe
now and healed, completely at peace and
filled with joy unspeakable! I do know that
God's ways are much higher than ours and He
is always working to fulfill a plan that is so much
greater than we could ever comprehend. I choose to
trust my son to the Father who is able to keep him for
me until I see him again.

Dear Father, You are so wise and so good. Your plans are always perfect. When I can't make sense out of all my pain and what has happened to my child help me to lean into Your faithful love and watch care over us. I praise You, Lord, for caring for me especially during this difficult season. Amen.

Day 33

2 Corinthians 4:16-18 "That is why we never give up. Though our bodies are dying, our spirits are being renewed every day. For our present troubles are small and won't last very long. Yet they produce for us a glory that vastly outweighs them and will last forever! So we don't look at the troubles we can see now; rather, we fix our gaze on things that cannot be seen. For the things we see now will soon be gone, but the things we cannot see will last forever" (NLT).

I'M STILL GRIEVING. It's not as intense as it was in the beginning but I'm still feeling the deep aching and if I allowed myself to I could easily slide down into that rabbit hole of continual sadness. However, I look up into the face of my Heavenly Father and I remember my hope! In my grief I can still hold on to the hope of being reunited with my child. The hope that God will continue to heal my broken heart to the point where I can live a life with joy. Hope that I will have more thoughts of peace and joy when I think of my son instead of sorrow.

I'm still grieving and it's okay. I'm slowly moving forward—that's good. But oh, so slowly. With such a huge loss I must allow myself all the time I need to express my grief for one I deeply loved—who was part of my very being.

Dear Father, please renew my hope in You and in what You say in Your Word. I stake my very life upon Your promises. Thank You for the promise of life after death. And that in the very end, the consummation of all things, everything will turn out to be okay. I place my trust in You and choose to keep my eyes on You. Amen.

Day 34

Psalm 40:2 "He brought me up also out of a horrible pit, out of the miry clay, and set my feet upon a rock, and established my steps" (KJ 2000)

TODAY I WOULD like you to try to take a break away from your major grief. What do I mean? I mean that when we are so completely absorbed with our loss and our feelings and emotions are completely off kilter we can lose perspective of life—our life and the lives of those around us. We can find ourselves caught in a dark rabbit hole and all we can see is the pain, the darkness, the sadness, the loss, the missing....

I remember one day I was alone at home and Ike was at work. I began to think about Joseph and tried to remember his presence, his laughter, and his words. I looked at his photos over and over again and you guessed it—I wailed away and just opened my mouth gasping with grief that was trying to suffocate me. I panicked and tried to get a hold of my grief mentors. No one was home. I tried to pray and began to speak out loud to myself telling myself that these moments would pass and I would make it through—others have been where I am right now and they made it through. I began to get my mind on something else. I told myself I would not allow myself to get that low in my grief ever again.

You see we have the control whether or not how long we stay in a grieving state or grief attack and how deep we allow ourselves to fall. If we feel like we are going crazy and cannot function we are allowing ourselves to go too deep. We have to have boundaries even in our grief. This doesn't mean we don't grieve, we do grieve and feel profoundly sad and we do feel the agonizing pain of our loss. However, we can allow ourselves to fall deeper down, down into that dark rabbit hole if we are not aware of what's happening.

I was heading deeper and deeper down this rabbit hole and it frightened me. Would I ever be able to come back out? Would I ever feel better? I felt I lost myself. Then God revealed to me what was happening. I pulled myself up and began to reread my grief books, the sections that spoke to my struggles of that moment. I encouraged myself. God gave me strength and then I took a *break* from my grief.

I watched a good movie, ate some ice cream, started to paint a new painting and *perspective* began to fall back into place.

Which perspective I would lose over and over again until I regained my inner balance—but never like that one day.

So when you feel you are slipping down that hole, stop and take a break. Do something that makes you feel good.

Dear Father, please help me to gain perspective as I am grieving. Steady my inner balance and emotions. Give me wisdom to know how to grieve and when my sorrow is dragging me down into that dark, deep hole. Show me what to do to get my mind on something else for a while so I can take a break from my pain. Amen.

Day 35

Hebrews 11:10 "Abraham was confidently looking forward to a city with eternal foundations, a city designed and built by God" (NLT).

D O YOU EVER wonder what your child is doing up in heaven? I do. I asked the Lord to give me some ideas.

The Bible tells us that when we become believers in the Lord Jesus Christ we are made unto Him Kings (Queens) and Priests (Revelation 1:6). In this age we are given that position but it will not be fully activated until Jesus returns to earth as ruling King over all. There we will rule and reign in His glorious kingdom with Him! We will have people and things to graciously rule over, judge, and bless. All this to say that I believe at this moment in heaven our children are learning the ways of the Kingdom they will be ruling. They are probably taking classes and studying under the King of Kings Himself. They may be learning many new things about heaven, the universe and the ages to come.

They also could be enjoying each other's company and talking about their days on earth—and their loved ones—that's you and me.

I can also see them playing their favorite sports, using their gifts and talents—blessing Jesus and each other. Believe me they are not sorrowing or worried about anything. They are completely whole in every way. There's a lot to do in their new home—heaven.

They will be excited to show us all what they've learned and how they have grown so we will be proud of them—even in heaven.

Dear Father, thank You for heaven! Thank You that my child is happy and whole in every way right this minute. Thank You that he/she has nothing to worry about but lives in joy and peace. Lord, give me a little dream or vision of what my child may be doing up there with You. Amen.

Day 36

John 11:25-26 *"I am the resurrection and the life. The one who believes in me will live, even though they die; and whoever lives by believing in me will never die. Do you believe this?"*

REMEMBER JESUS SAID this statement in the Bible.

Do you believe this? I do.

God wants us to grab hold of life and live abundantly now in this age and then live forever in the age to come. Jesus is that Life—He, Himself is Life Eternal.

Place your trust in Him. Release your child to His care and love. Know that God loves your child with

a love that is so large it can't ever fill up the skies. Then walk and live in His strength. He's there and if you call upon Him He will give you the desperately needed strength for each moment you are alive. Hold on to the life line of God and allow it to pull you forward into peace of mind, inner joy, and life itself.

"With God all things are possible." This means we can and will make it through this valley of grief and loss.

Dear Father, pull me forward towards life. Towards the life that is before me. Thank You that You are my life in this life and in the next. Help me to embrace life each time it presents itself. *Amen.*

Day 37

Psalm 71:20-21 "Though you have made me see troubles, many and bitter, you will restore my life again; from the depths of the earth you will again bring me up. You will increase my honor and comfort me once more."

I AM BEGINNING TO accept the truth much more these days. My child is not coming back to me on this earth. I can't change that but I can change the way I see things and I can allow this tragedy to change me in positive ways. This sure doesn't happen overnight.

I feel I am turning another corner in my grief journey. There are so many corners. I'm working on accepting my loss even if I don't like it. The truth is my boy is gone. Now what will I do? Profoundly grieve and let the tears flow until I feel it's time to move on a little more. I will always remember this huge truth from other grieving moms who have survived and are enjoying life again. We must go *through* the pain in order to come *through* to the other side of grief which is acceptance and reinvesting our lives purposefully.

But we are not alone. We can get the support we

need from other moms who've lost a child, from grief groups, our church, family and friends.

As you know very well losing a child creates such a deep hole in our hearts. We ache so badly in missing them. Only God can heal our hearts—remember He said He would. "I will heal the broken in heart and bind up their wounds" (Psalm 147:3).

My heart is healing. I can feel it. That's part of the corner I'm turning. However, I will never be surprised when I am reminded of my Joseph by a place, a thing, a person, music, aromas, that it surely at times will cause tears to flow.

We will heal but we will always miss our child. We will never forget.

Dear Father, thank You for bringing healing into my life. Give me the strength to continue to hold steady and to work through my days of grief and pain. Hold me close to You and let me be more aware of Your presence with me. Continue to lead me to those people, places and things that will help me to heal and be restored. Amen.

Day 38

Luke 2:19 "but Mary kept all these things in her heart and thought about them often" (NLT).

WHAT ARE SOME of the things you did with your child that you will always be glad you did and never regret it? We don't expect them to die before us so I know there are lots of "I wish I had done this or that." But there are some things we did do that we can forever treasure.

I can remember some nights I would pick up Joseph from his crib and dance around the room with him looking right into his twinkling eyes. We danced to the music of a lullaby. I remember taking a snapshot in my mind of those moments—I wanted them to stay forever. That snapshot is still with me. My baby son was so delighted to dance with me.

I know there are many parenting books out now that say we are not to pick up our baby whenever they cry—sometimes we need

to let them cry them-
selves to sleep. Joseph was
different. I chose to pick him up *every* time he
cried. I would hold him close and quiet his fears and
tears. I'll never regret it. I loved him then and I love
him now.

Dear Father, thank You that I had precious times with my child. If there were things I should have done or not to have done I place these all in Your hand. Help me to focus on the beautiful memories that You allowed me to have. I love my child so much. Thank You for keeping them safe with You. Amen.

Day 39

Proverbs 16:24 "Kind words are like honey— sweet to the soul and healthy for the body" (NLT).

AT THE BEGINNING of my grief journey it was impossible for me to believe that I would ever feel better—especially to the point of enjoying life again. My heart was so deeply crushed I had to do everything I could to hold on to my sanity and not allow myself to slide way down into the dark enveloping abyss that was there just waiting for me.

If some of you are going through this beginning season of your grief please take heart. The things I learned that have helped me so very much I think will help you too. Here they are:

1. Keep your faith in God, in His love, strength and comfort. Pray. Talk to God about it all.

2. Find Scriptures from the Bible that encourage you.

3. Learn from others who have come through to the other side of grief.

4. Share your story over and over with safe and trustworthy people.

5. Work on your grief by understanding it and the stages, by feeling your feelings and not running or hiding from them—rather going through them. Develop a healthy perspective of what you are experiencing.

6. When you are ready get involved helping others with the gifts God has given you.

These things have kept me sane and helped me through my most difficult moments.

Remember you are deeply loved whether it feels like it or not.

Dear Father, give me the ability and strength to work on my grief a little each day as it comes up. Help me to continue to have the courage to work through my painful feelings and dark days. Show me how to use my faith in You to keep my broken heart steady. Help me to get up when I fall. Direct me to where I can use the gifts You have given me. Amen.

Day 40

Philippians 4:13 "I can do all this through him who gives me strength."

ALWAYS REMEMBER THAT the feelings of the moment will pass. When you are feeling overwhelmed with your sadness and pain, remember that these feelings—the intensity of them will not last forever. They are feelings of the moment. We can stand anything for a period of time. These feelings and emotions come and they will go just like the contractions of a birthing mother who brings a child into the world. Do not be fooled into believing your emotions will never change and that you can't stand the state you may find your-self in. The truth is your emotions will change and you can stand anything moment by moment with God's grace and strength. This way of thinking has been one of my chief building blocks that I use in building my founda-tion of life. Remember what you are saying to yourself is very important—replace lies with truth. Don't deny what is true but allow it just to be as you speak gently to yourself—you will make it through this time in your life.

God loves you and of course I love you. We are moms together with a common bond.

Dear Father, my emotions have been like a roller coaster sometimes and I am afraid of losing control of myself. Please open my eyes to the truth in Your Word that tells me I will make it through no matter how difficult it becomes. You said "I will walk through the valley of the shadow of death and I would fear no evil." I choose to believe that I am strong in You and that I will have victory even in my grief and sadness. Show me how, Dear Lord. *Amen.*

Day 41

Psalm 62:1-2 "Truly my soul finds rest in God; my salvation comes from him. Truly he is my rock and my salvation; he is my fortress, I will never be shaken."

THE OTHER DAY I was in the grocery store and a young man, about my son's age, was helping with my groceries. After wards I told him he was the best and because he was so new on the job, I also told him he would continue to do an excellent job.

As I pushed my cart out of the store I thought of my own son and how that could have been him, a young man working in a grocery store. I remembered my son's kindness and gentle demeanor and I began to weep all the way to the car. I sobbed my heart out for it would never be so—that I would get to praise him for the jobs he would do. When I pulled into the garage I just sat in the car with tears falling and tissues flying. My son, my son.

The next day when I awoke in the morning I felt better. I wasn't filled with sadness. I thought to myself, "What makes one day better than the other in our grief journey?" I believe how we feel physically has a direct affect with how our emotions behave. And how we feel has quite a bit to do with what we are thinking about.

On a bad day everything has a dark edge—fears and worries are exaggerated—that hopelessness feeling creeps up. And so the struggle begins again to stay afloat and to try to maintain any emotional stability we have. It is on these days I cling to God and search His Word for more understanding, strength and comfort—all I can do at times is just be with Him leaning on Him.

On a good day I have a sense of peace. My lot in life is more acceptable and workable. I see for sure the silver lining in the cloud. I feel God close to me. My faith is much steadier and I just feel good.

Now the conclusion is that I am learning that whether it's a good day or bad day God never changes and He is always close to me. The silver lining has always been there. And my faith is still my solid ground on which to stand—it's not shifting sand.

So as we go through our good days and bad days remember all the good has always been and is always there it just takes time to realize this and in knowing this brings a peace that we will always, always make it through.

Dear Father, on my bad days help me to walk by faith and choose to believe that You are still with me. That You are still directing my paths and that You love me. On my good days put a new song in my mouth even praise to You! Whether I feel it or not You have promised to give me just what I need for today. I choose to walk in Your promises. Amen.

Day 42

Ecclesiastes 3:4 "A time to weep and a time to laugh, a time to mourn and a time to dance."

I F YOU ARE feeling that you just can't keep going on and life is too hard— Please listen this is for you.

No matter how difficult and impossible it may seem right now it will not always be that way. Seasons change. This is the time to mourn but there will come a time to dance! Don't ever give up hope or listen in to thoughts that make life darker for you. Look up because your redemption draws near in God.

You will indeed make it through each and every episode of grief and tears. I can vouch for this because I have and am experiencing it in my own life. God's grace and strength are truly sufficient. Tell yourself this. Talk gently to yourself. Your loss has given you a heavy blow. It has knocked you flat on your face. It's been a huge ordeal that has unmercifully left you without strength. I know. I've been there.

Tell yourself that these days that are so hard will pass. Live in the moment because you will find all you need right here. You will not go crazy. You will live again. God said you will.

Keep taking those small but steady steps. Keep walking through your grief and let the tears fall. This is all part of your healing. There will come a time when you are not all consumed with your pain. Yes there will.

Dear Father, please keep hope alive in my heart during hard times. Remind me that I am healing as I purposely take one step at a time forward. As I refuse to be cast down deep into that abyss of darkness. But, and if, I slip down I am confident that You will always, always pull me out. Amen.

Day 43

*Romans 11:33-34 "Who can measure the
wealth and wisdom and knowledge of God?
Who can understand his decisions or explain
what he does? Has anyone known the thoughts
of the Lord or given him advice" (CEV)?*

AN WE TRUST in the wisdom of God? Does He
know what is best for us and our loved ones?
Does He ever make a mistake? Can we trust
His wisdom and purpose in the death of our child?

The Bible tells us that God's wisdom is so far
beyond what we can ever fathom. His ways are past
finding out. He created us so we can trust that He
knows what we need before we even ask Him. God
purposes what He will do and allow in our lives and
in our loved one's life in order to fulfill His eternal
plans. Nothing escapes His eye or surprises Him when
it happens. Immediately He begins to work out something positive into our lives from the negative circumstances that have turned our lives upside down.

When we found out that our child had died one of
the first questions we may have asked is why? Where
was God? What's going on? In God's infinite wisdom
He has carefully prepared and planned the very

moment our child would leave this earth. However, it is a shock to us.

Over the past months I have come to realize how wise God is and I can now even thank Him for bringing my son into His presence absent from all pain and suffering. I trust God's wisdom in my life and in the lives of those I love. There is always a clear purpose for loss of a child—which purpose only God really knows.

<h1 style="text-align:center">Day 44</h1>

*Psalm 116:8 "For you, LORD, have deliv-
ered me from death, my eyes from
tears, my feet from stumbling."*

I AM REJOICING TODAY! I see a promising future ahead! I see glimpses of where God is taking me. I am rising out of the ashes—He is raising me up from the dead! Is this possible after such a tragic horrendous happening in my life? Yes.

I keep saying that God is the One who will heal our broken hearts and He will and does. Overnight? No. There are things we learn along the way—there will always be things to learn. I am so happy (if that's okay?) to use all that God has given me to bless humanity. It's so satisfying. That's how my day is today. I don't know what tomorrow will bring but I know now for sure that I will make it through that bad day and keep rising like a cloud into a huge sky of dreams and promises.

Will you rise with me? Little by little? If I could I would take you by the hand and bring you along with me—in a sense that is just what I am doing in these times of interaction.

You don't see a happy future? Don't worry things

change. They always change and it is best if we work to change with them. You will make it to that light at the end of the tunnel. Keep your eyes open and you will see glimpses of the light rays every now and then as you continue your upward ascent. Love you.

Dear Father, praise You for the gifts You have placed within me to share with humanity. Thank You that Your promises are sure and strong. I never have to be afraid of tomorrow because You will be there to carry and support me. You will pick me up on Your eagle wings and cause me one day to soar above the clouds. Amen.

Day 45

1 John 4:16 "And so we know and rely on the love God has for us. God is love. Whoever lives in love lives in God, and God in them."

As I was taking a nap I thought about my beautiful son, Joseph and yearned to be with him. Missing him is so hard. Then I felt a warm feeling in my heart and remembered that I had his love in there deep down. I remembered that Jesus' love filled up my heart and then there was that special little place where Joe's love lived on because he lived on with Jesus.

Love is not a tangible thing but we can see its effects and feel it can't we? Love, I believe is a spiritual essence from the heart of God given to us to give to each other and back to God.

When I think of my son and his love for me I can feel that love residing inside me— it is a promise to me that we will meet again someday. We will again dance with joy and happiness!

Day 46

I HAVE FOUND THAT developing and cultivating a thankful and grateful heart even in times of great sorrow is healing in itself. We cannot forget the blessings we do have—even the time we had our dear child with us is to be thankful for. When I find myself ruminating over how much I miss my son I can hear God whispering to my heart, "What about the precious and sweet times you enjoyed with him? He was the joy of your heart and still is!"

What a treasure to have memories to think back upon no matter how long or short they were—they are ours to hold dear to our hearts forever.

We can choose to be grateful for those days, those moments. Thank you, Jesus, for the miracle of my son!

Dear Father, I lift my voice up to You and thank You with all of my heart for choosing and blessing me to become a mother. Thank You for my beloved child that I so treasure. Thank You for the joys and even the sorrows of being a mother. You are so good to me. Amen.

Day 47

Proverbs 27:17 "As iron sharpens iron so a friend encourages and revives his friend's heart by the comforting and encouraging words he speaks" (Eilers' Paraphrase).

EVERY TIME I share the personal story of my grief it brings a little bit more healing to my heart. We cannot be afraid to share our feelings and stories about our loved one because we think everyone is tired of hearing them. We need to find those who we know love us and care about our loss. Sometimes they also have to learn to grow being patient and loving as they listen again and again. Be who you are at the moment and if that means you want to share something about your child then do it. If the response is negative then don't hang out with that person when you want to talk about your beloved. Depending on how close your relationship is you can tell them how their reaction makes you feel—this gives them the chance to change and be more sensitive to your heart.

I have just about always had good reactions when sharing my story and memories of Joe with friends. If I feel they are tired of hearing about my grief I don't share it with those particular friends. But more than not our friends care and want us to feel we can talk to them. Sometimes they are afraid to bring up our child for fear that it will make us feel pain and produce tears—but we have to tell them that it's okay for us to remember and feel deeply.

I am gratefully thankful to all of those dear ones who have held my hand and listened to the same stories over and over again and who have loved me in my tears and fears. What would I do without you? My heart has received much comfort and healing.

Dear Father, please continue to bring into my life the dear people who will be willing to listen to my story again and again. Thank You for those You have brought to me. Help me to remember to thank them personally for being there for me. Amen.

Day 48

Psalm 73:26 "My health may fail, and my spirit may grow weak, but God remains the strength of my heart; he is mine forever" (NLT).

GRIEF IS VERY exhausting because it drains our emotions and emotional reserves. When I first started on my grief journey it seemed all I did was sleep. My husband would help me with the housework plus do his own job of driving the taxi. I was just too tired not only emotionally but mentally, physically and spiritually. It's been over three years now and I'm just starting to get my energy back. However, I take naps and am not working outside the house. I need to know my limits and just how much I can take emotionally in a situation.

As grieving moms we must take care of ourselves. We are not robots and we do have limitations on our bodies and minds. Rest much and soak in God's mercy and love. Give Him your burdens each time you lay your head on your pillow. Take easy slow steps to your healing. Do what you can and know when you are over doing it. Say no when you need to.

I've had to turn down invitations to do some things because I knew it would be too much at this time in my season of grief. I have said yes to some things. Yes to helping other moms. Yes to using my gifts and talents. Yes to spending time with friends and family—but watching to reserve my strength. Yes to walking when I'm up to it. Yes to thinking about my son but also knowing when emotionally it is too taxing. Yes to loving and being with my husband.

I want to live free from stress as much as possible.

As I increase and grow stronger I will choose what things I want to add to my life. One thing I've learned is I am responsible to give myself self care. If I take good care of myself I can give out more to others who need it.

Each of us recovers at our own pace.

Dear Father, show me the areas that I need to pull back on that are taxing my strength. Help me not to be afraid to say I can't do something when I feel I can't. Bring some balance back into my life. Help me to make wise choices every day. Please, Lord, sustain me spiritually, mentally and physically. Show me how to rest and nurture myself so I can keep on moving towards healing. Amen.

Day 49

1 Peter 5:7 "Casting all your cares on him, because he cares about you" (Christian Standard Bible).

I PULLED OUT SOME old photographs of days past with my son, Joseph. I laughed and cried and treasured each memory as I studied each photo. Those days were good, but some were difficult as my Joe got older and suffered with bipolar illness. But good or difficult I valued every single minute with him.

Photos can bring us back to those moments we shared with our child. They can stir up our hearts and emotions as we try to grasp what was and what will never be again. It cannot be fully comprehended—the fact that our child was here and was so alive and so deeply knitted into our hearts. Now they are away living in their new home with Jesus in heaven, a wondrous place that we are not permitted to enter until the time is right. Our place up there is being prepared for us as we live and learn on this earth.

I pray daily, "Lord teach me how to live without my son." It is never an easy deal but rather at times very frustrating, confusing, heart wrenching to say the least. But this I know, that God has our children and us in His tender care—for whether we live we live unto the Lord and whether we die we die unto the Lord. Whether we live or die we are the Lord's.

This I know that He is faithful to teach us how to live our lives here on earth without our child by our side.

I am learning—slowly and painfully. I am moving ahead one step at a time.

Dear Father, continue to guide my life and teach me each day how to live without my child with me. Give me new ideas, new plans, new hopes and dreams. Ignite the flicker of hope within my heart. Lead me forward. Steady my wobbly steps. Help me to find my life and satisfaction in You. Put Your desires in my heart and mind. Thank You, Lord. Amen.

Day 50

Philippians 2:4 "Don't look out only for your own interests, but take an interest in others, too" (NLT).

Today I was honored to speak at a *Grief Share* group. What a joy to encourage others who have also lost a loved one. I love to be used by God to bless others. Their stories have helped me bring even more perspective to my own.

This is one of the things that I have learned that brings healing into our lives—reaching out to others when you can and are ready.

We get our minds off of our own loss even if for a little while. We learn we are not alone and that others hurt also. God can use our pain to help and encourage others. He can work the ugliness of our loss for good—out of death comes life—life for us and for those who need it. My Joe did not die in vain. The story of his life and death are reaching many who need hope, who need to know there is still a God who cares and loves.

If my suffering can bring hope and strength to someone it makes it all worth it. It is not wasted. God will use your story also as you heal and grow stronger on your grief journey. But first you must have your time to really grieve your great loss—the horrific loss of your child. We loved deeply and so we must grieve deeply.

Day 51

Psalm 62:8 "Trust in him at all times, you people; pour out your hearts to him, for God is our refuge."

I THINK ONE OF the most difficult things about losing a child is how much they are missed in our daily lives. There is such an emptiness without them that at times it is very hard to bear. We ache for them—to hear their voice and see their face again— or to be able to say goodbye. Missing their presence is the one thing that can open the wound over and over again. How can we ever heal?

What God is teaching me at this time in my grief journey is to hand Him my brokenness. In those moments of heart-wrenching longing for our loved one we can pour out our soul before God. He listens and hears our cries. Not only does He hear but He promises to do something about them. As we press into Him with each painful moment and memory that arises and ask Him to fill that void, I believe a little more healing comes to our wounded soul. I truly believe that when God tells us that He will heal our hearts and bind up our wounds that He will do it. Of course it takes time because there are stages we have to process through— there are layers of pain to be healed.

Even if our wound seems to re-open each time we feel that pang of loss we learn how to give it to God so He can pour in His healing oil of the Holy Spirit. Each time we have a choice to stay in that sadness and melancholy state or we can feel it, process it, lay it before God and then take some steps to move forward a little more. Yes we can heal if we want to. But let us first do our grieving and then when we are ready we can move towards joining life again.

One day we will find that even though we still miss our child greatly it does not control our life, because we will know we will see them again and that this separation is temporary. We will find that peace and purpose have taken the place of the pain.

Dear Father, I press into Your love today. I lean into You. Soothe my aching heart that so misses my child. Give me strength to make the choice to feel my pain when it comes. Then to process it and lay it out before You. Show me even how to grieve. Cover me today with Your presence and power. Amen.

Day 52

*Jeremiah 29:11 "For I know the plans I
have for you," declares the LORD, "plans
to prosper you and not to harm you,
plans to give you hope and a future."*

THERE IS ALWAYS a purpose for things happening in our lives—I believe this. Even when we can't make any sense out of what is happening or has happened. Like the death of our child.

There is always a plan and a purpose in God, our Creator's mind. We think death is the worst thing that can happen to our child and if we look at it with only our human eyes, it is. But do we know how happy they are? Do we know how full of peace they are? It is not bad for them, for they are basking in the perfect love of God with those in heaven. We, on the other hand, are seeing only with our human eyes and we see no one where someone used to be. This is where our faith can help us.

Do we really believe they are made whole and full of joy? This thought can bring us comfort because it is true. For our child who departs from this world is immediately present with Jesus. We must try to see with the other eyes we have—the eyes of faith. God is bigger than the universe He created and His purposes are always perfect, upright and done in loving kindness. Can we be at peace trusting our child to His arms of safety?

Now there is a purpose and a plan for our lives in having to experience such pain, sorrow and grief. Step by step, I believe, as we begin to heal, and include God in our healing, we will begin to see our purpose. His plan however is at times beyond our understanding in the whole scope of things. His design is beautiful. Can we also trust Him with this? We do know that He tells us in the Bible that His plans are never to bring us harm but to give us a hopeful future.

Dear Father, help me to see what Your plans are for me. Show me my purpose. Give me the grace to trust You with the destiny of my child. You are good, wise, merciful and loving. I choose to put my trust in You and not to fear—for my future or for my child. Thank You for loving me and for taking care of my child. Amen.

Day 53

Psalm 139:1-3 "You have searched me, LORD, and you know me. You know when I sit and when I rise; you perceive my thoughts from afar. You discern my going out and my lying down; you are familiar with all my ways."

I'M LEARNING NEVER to calculate my grief journey without God. We can never leave God out of the equation. This grief journey was never meant to be traveled alone. By ourselves, in our own strength we cannot fully heal our broken heart. Only the One who created our heart can fully heal it. If we let Him He will show us how to work with Him in bringing about our healing. He will bring people into our lives that we need just at the right moment. We are not in this alone. We may feel very alone at times, but it just isn't true. There is always hope and always a light ahead for us.

Sometimes we lose perspective because of our sorrow and we cannot see anything good or happy—we feel hopeless. Where is God when I keep on suffering with this pain?

God is with you in your pain. Remember Jesus experienced in some way all the things we would ever have to face on earth. He understands loss. He hates when our loved ones and friends leave us through death. His desire is that we would never have to die but because of our sin death has passed on to each of us. The good news is that this separation between us and our loved ones does not have to be permanent for Jesus made the way for us all to live again. When we place our faith in Christ we are guaranteed to keep on living. First in our spiritual body and then in our newly resurrected body at the day when all the dead will be raised. These are not just fairy tales. Jesus wants us to know our hope is sure and steadfast so we have hope in this life. Hope for our loved ones who pass on.

If we include God in our sorrow He will bring us out because He promised to. Even then grief is still a journey we all must walk at sometime—but not alone.

Dear Father, thank You that You made a way for us to be reunited with our child. I believe that You have made Yourself known to my child at some time and that they have chosen to be with You. You will not lose one of our little ones.

Father, I want to include You in my sorrow. I need You so desperately every day to sustain me. Let me be more aware of Your presence today. Amen.

Day 54

John 14:1-2 *"Jesus said, 'Let not your heart be troubled, you believe in God believe also in me. In my Father's house are many mansions. I go to prepare a place for you. And if I go and prepare a place for you I will come again and receive you unto myself that where I am there you will be also."*

I WAS JUST THINKING about Joe and I realized once again that I would not be seeing him any time soon here on planet earth. He has left this temporary home and has gone to live with his Father God in heaven the place where Jesus said He was preparing for each of us a special home. The Bible calls it a "mansion!" Wow! Each possessing a beautiful mansion! I wonder what Joe's mansion looks like? I'm sure it is everything and more than he's ever wanted, desired and dreamed. I remember him telling me when he got to heaven he wanted to have a pet dinosaur and singing little fancy rats dressed up in tiny suits. Well with God everything is possible!

One thing that really makes me happy is that I know my son is safe and cared for by the One who loves him most and created him. No more sorrow or suffering. No more struggles with sin and evil. God is so

gracious and good. I think we can safely
say that the departure of our loved one
was one that was planned beforehand
by God in order to bring them into
the wonders of the wonderful place
with Himself. He wanted them to
be where He was probably because
He knew they would be completely
happy and whole.

When I think of Joe filled with joy up
there—really not far from us all—it makes
me want to go on with my life and be content
while I am here. He would want me to be. When the
time comes for my departure it will be as if no time
has passed at all since I last saw him. It will be a
continuation of our relationship with only the good,
happy and joyful to relish in.

Dear Father, thank You for heaven! I choose to believe that my child is so happy with You up there. No more pain or sorrow. I also choose to work on being more content here on earth living the rest of my days wisely and preparing myself for heaven. Your joy is my strength so I rejoice in You today. Amen.

Day 55

*Ecclesiastes 3:3 "…a time to tear
down and a time to build."*

As a mom who has lost a child there comes a time when we begin to rebuild our life. We decide we must survive and learn to live with our grief because it is part of our life now. We can't pretend it never happened. We know it happened. But we don't want to stay frozen in the broken state forever—there is hope after loss.

As we work through our grief, what we learn becomes stepping stones to be walked upon that will lead us to another path bringing us on a new journey. Yes our loss will always be with us in our secret place but we must learn to live without our child with us. And I believe we can by taking one of these steps at a time.

As we keep walking we will begin to see that the scenery around us is beginning to change—or is it that we are looking at it with different eyes now? Then after a while we see in the distance the sun beginning to rise, glistening through the trees. The world is awakening all around us—or is it that we are coming alive again?

One of the most difficult things in this lifetime is having to live without our child. I believe we can if we take the risks and choices to move forward. I believe we can if we hold to God's hand. He promises to lead us and He can't lie.

We are here. We still live on this beautiful planet earth and we've got a lot to accomplish yet.

Dear Father, teach me and help me to rebuild my life and to live my life without my child. Bring joy back into my beaten heart and restore my soul. Each time I work on my grief help me to use what I learn as a stepping stone to bring me closer to my new life I must live. Amen.

Day 56

Ecclesiastes 3:1 "There is a time for everything, and a season for every activity under the heavens."

I HATED TO HEAR that phrase "my new normal." I wanted my old normal self not this person who felt lost, confused and out of place. I didn't feel like I fit in anywhere except my grief groups. Everyone was going about their daily routine life when my world had been bulldozed over. What is this "new normal?" I learned that wording from grief group and grief books. All I knew was who I had been and wasn't any more. So I began to search for my new normal. Who was I? What would my life be like now? I was still Ike's wife. Still a woman who loved God and who God loved. Still a woman who had gifts and talents. Still a woman who loved people. I could go on. But my role as a mother was completely changed. My life had previously revolved around my only son, Joseph. Now he was gone. I actually felt I lost something—something was missing in my life. That's why I felt so lost because I couldn't find what I lost.

Day by day passed and I slowly crawled about processing the huge changes in my life. New normal. The new me. A new role. I can't go into all that I had to process and experience in order to find my place. I decided to focus my life around God knowing and loving Him more—building a deeper relationship. I found solace in my painting and writing. My relationship with my husband grew closer and deeper. People at the church loved on me. My grief group friends supported me. Then I found a niche—at least for now. That was to minister to others who had also lost a child. I decided to use my days to rest and pace myself in order to heal. I began to take better care of myself—began to experience some joy and contentment. I love life a little more. I am gradually finding my new normal.

It is not something you find over night. It is a process and a journey in itself. With God at the helm we will find that place where we become more comfortable with ourselves and our life.

Dear Father, please help me to continue to find my new normal life. Help me to continue to build my life around You and Your plans and purpose for me. I choose to take care of myself as I am walking through my grief. Please open my eyes to the person that You are so patiently transforming me into. Amen.

Day 57

GOD IS SO big and so capable of taking care of His children who are sorrowing deeply over their great loss. He has been drawing me close to His heart during this journey of grief I've been walking. He has been calling you to draw near to Him as He is drawing near to you already. There in the huge heart of God we can find the consolation we so desperately need. We can find hope and a love that cries when we cry and laughs when we laugh. He knows those very impossible moments that we must pass through and He is with us in them too.

God is so big He wants to take care of all our needs. He doesn't want us to worry or fear. We never wanted our child to fear or worry. We wanted them to feel safe and cared for. So that is how our big God is and more exceedingly.

Jesus said we are to pray and say, "Our Father, who art in heaven…." He's our Daddy. If you want to know what the Father God is like just look at Jesus. Jesus also said that "He who has seen me has seen the Father." Not one *like* the Father, but the Father Himself.

Jesus was gentle, good, forgiving, unselfish, caring, compassionate, providing. He never lied but was Himself the embodiment of Truth. He proclaimed to be the Messiah—the Chosen One sent from God to save the world. We just have to believe in Him to enter into the huge heart of the Father. God is big enough to take care of you and me. Can we curl up into His presence and find all we need in Him?

Dear Father, I call you Father. I curl up by faith into Your arms of love. I hide in You. Cover me as I sit here in You. Cover my brokenness and fill my empty heart with a fresh hope. Abba, Daddy, Father, I am Your daughter and I love You. Amen.

Day 58

Matthew 11:28-29 "Come to me, all you who are weary and burdened, and I will give you rest. Take my yoke upon you and learn from me, for I am gentle and humble in heart, and you will find rest for your souls."

SOMETIMES I THINK I've turned a corner in my grief journey and so I have. Other times I think I have turned that corner—but I haven't. It has led me back to a place I thought I had come out of.

You can't rush grief. It will have its way. It takes its time and when we rush it or hide from it, it will somehow manage to make itself known when we least

expect it. It is up the hill, down in the valley, across the land, through the rocky places, stumbling into some pot holes. Falling on our face and getting back up again.

Grief hurts. It is very uncomfortable but we won't die because of it. These emotions are in the depths of our souls and are to be processed and healed. We search within ourselves and we find somewhere to put this thought and that feeling where it can make some sense to us.

Grief doesn't define who we are. It is something we experience when we lose someone we love or something we value. It is a built in deal. We were created this way. We lose—we grieve. But how we learn to navigate through it is important so that we are not going through life maimed.

I believe when we allow God to be a major source in the healing of our grief we are on the best road possible. When we learn all we can about our grief we will not be tossed about as much but have some sure footing.

God promises to bring us through this valley of the shadow of death—one moment at a time, one step at a time, and one day at a time. We will make it through and we will find our way.

Dear Father, please help me to navigate through my grief in a healthy way. Give me wisdom to know what to do when the pain sweeps me away. Help me to remember that grief is not who I am, but it is something I am going through and experiencing. Heal me, O God, and I shall be healed. Amen.

Day 59

Psalm 27:13 "I remain confident of this: I will see the goodness of the LORD in the land of the living."

I WAS THINKING TO myself as I was missing Joseph so very much. I know I have his memories from the past. I know I will see him in the future. But what about now? How do I handle this ache of "missing" him? I live in the present and that is what I have to deal with—my today, my now. I sent up a prayer and asked God how do I keep from being swallowed up and cast into a mode of lingering sadness when I long so for Joseph?

I just wanted my son close to me and physically here. How could I keep going on like this with the constant ache in my heart?

I could hear God say to me to feel the "missing" feelings and pass through those moments. Then to begin to recite my own purposes here on earth. It's all in our mindset.

When we switch
our focus on to some-
thing we have control over, this brings some
peace and stability into our lives. We cannot do anything about our child being gone—we can't bring
them back. But we can do the things that God has
placed in our hearts even if it means stepping out into
the unknown of doing something new.

We will always miss our beloved child but we cannot
allow it to dominate our thinking forever. We must
live again.

Dear Father, when I feel that familiar ache deep down in my heart for my child, give me strength to pass through it and not run from it. Help me to see what else I can focus on in the moments following so I will not lose perspective in my pain. Please tell my child that I miss them so very much and that I love them. Amen.

Day 60

Exodus 33:14 "The LORD replied, 'My Presence will go with you, and I will give you rest.'"

WHAT DO WE do with our fragile, broken, wounded hearts? The brokenness is real—our hearts are fragmented and must be restored and made whole again. Sometimes they hurt and ache so bad that we think we will lose our minds. We can't stand another minute of such pain on our tender bleeding hearts. It's scary, it's overwhelming, it's all consuming, it's crippling, it's so, so very deep, it's so unbearably sad. It's grief. It is also normal, human and temporary.

When we feel stuck and all we can pay attention to is the present tearing, searing agony that chokes our hearts we cannot stay there for a long time. We will make ourselves ill if we do. I'm not saying to ignore our feelings and brokenness—no we feel it and allow ourselves to pass *through* it for we must do this in order to heal. However, we don't want to park our car there. How do we change our focus?

Tonight I was listening to my son playing his guitar and singing with me on my phone recorder. All of a sudden I was gripped inside with desperateness and all

I could see was endless loss and pain. What could I do? I had to do what I tell other moms to do. I pressed and leaned into the presence and love of my God. I asked Him to continue to heal my brokenness and to help me to refocus. I thanked Him for taking care of my son and that my son was safe, whole and happy. I reminded myself that this pain will not last forever—it gets better and I will see my Joe again.

By the time my husband got home I had steadied my heart and was looking forward to sharing with you.

My heart goes out to all of you who are suffering so. It is so hard but don't lose heart. Speak kindly to yourself and tell yourself it's okay to have these feelings of grief and you will get through moment by moment.

Dear Father, I don't like this pain and sorrow. I don't like this darkness and despair that grips my heart at times. Sometimes I feel sick. O God, direct my thoughts towards the present where I am and what I am doing. Bring me back to reality. In the confusion of my thoughts You bring me back to stability. Direct my heart to tend to those who need me now, today. Amen.

Day 61

Psalm 139:13 "You made all the delicate, inner parts of my body and knit me together in my mother's womb" (NLT).

MY HUSBAND, IKE, and I were married nineteen years before we had our beloved son. Why did we wait so long? You'll have to read my first book to exactly know why. My book is *Hope in a Season of Suffering*. But to put it in a nutshell I did not feel emotionally ready to raise a child. After working through many fears and trepidation, plus now that I was 39 years old, I knew it was now or never. I always wanted a baby and prayed daily about it. I prayed earnestly for the precious baby I would be carrying and delivering into the world. God was with me.

When Joe was born I was overcome with awe—why had I waited so long to have him? Immediately we were bonded forever. I fell in love with my infant son. My husband was speechless as he helped deliver Joe. He would be a good father that Joe would need. But I was his MOM. My relationship to and with him would be so different and unique than what he and Ike would have. (Ike would have to tell you how much he loved and loves his boy.)

Truly Joseph was a gift to both of us—a joyful gift—a ball of pure energy and delight! I am so glad we took so many photos of all his stages while growing up. Little did I know those photos would be all I would have left to remember our times together.

If you have photos and feel like you can, go through each one and recall that day, that time, that feeling, your child's personality—what you shared. Sometimes it will make you cry. Other times it will make you laugh.

Aren't you so very glad and thankful you were able to be a mom to your precious child?

Dear Father, thank You again for the gift of my child. Thank You for cameras so that photos could be taken of my child for keepsakes. I can relive those memories—at least for a few moments in time. Thank You for the part of my brain that can remember. I rejoice over my child and sing praise to You, my God! Amen.

Day 62

*Psalm 127:3 "Children are a gift from the
LORD; they are a reward from him" (NLT).*

I CAN'T THANK GOD enough for giving me the privilege of being a mother. I was 39 years old when
I had my son. It seems I waited all my life for a
child of my own. My darling baby boy.

Joe filled my life with such joy and then at times
with sorrow but he was the heavenly gift that God
allowed me to bring into this world. My life is different because I had him. My life is different because
I lost him. My life is being transformed because
he lived. My life is richer, deeper,
and fuller because of the love
between me and my son. My
life is becoming expectant—
I'm look anxiously to the day I
find him in heaven. Even though
it has been a huge loss for me when
my son left, he was found to be with
God— brought into his rightful home.

I am glad Joe lived. I love him so
much. I am relieved that he is safe and
deeply loved where he is. Just imagine

one day we will once again have fun being together in the next life, enjoying each other's company, telling stories about our lives on earth.

Aren't you glad you were given the joy and blessing of being a mom? Right now cherish the love of your child that you hold in your heart—because it is there—love never dies. God, who is pure awesome love Himself, holds you and your child. Always turn to Him and believe Him for He holds the words of life and happiness.

I know for some of you these days have been difficult. Keep holding to your hope—the God who loves you will heal your broken, torn and bruised heart.

Dear Father, thank You for the love of my child. Thank You that each day I am one day closer to seeing my child again. I believe in You and I believe Your Word. I choose to trust my life and my loss to You. Thank You for bringing me this far in my grief journey. I will hope in You and will not be disappointed. Amen.

Day 63

Psalm 18:6 "In my distress I called to the LORD; I cried to my God for help. From his temple he heard my voice; my cry came before him, into his ears."

Ouch! This hurts!

Grief truly does hurt emotionally and physically.

I was sorting through boxes in my garage getting rid of the stuff we don't need so when it is time to move to a new home we will be ready. And so it happened as I expected—a box of items belonging to my son. Birthday cards, baby book, trophies, tooth fairy notes from Mom and more. What should I keep? What should I let go of? There were things from his birth to young adult hood. Then there was the bent house key that my sister and I found that was thrown from his pocket when he got hit by that car—along with his broken glasses. Memories sweet and terrible.

Oh Joe, my Joe how I miss you. Then the familiar pain stole into my heart bringing with it tears. "This really hurts." I said. For a minute or so the shock of my loss came back and I almost couldn't believe it although I knew it was true. I had a son—these items were his—he was here—I was his mother. Now he is in a different place. What was my new perspective? I fumbled through the pages in my mind to find it so I could steady my heart. Oh yes—as I wiped my eyes. My son is no longer in the past—these are memories of him. He is alive in my future waiting for me. I deeply treasure all our memories and have hidden them down in my heart but I keep my focus on seeing him again and finishing my purpose here on earth.Sure memory stirs up pain but it will not control my life.

We have a life to live—our child would want us to.

Dear Father, as past memories fill my heart help me to keep perspective on where I am today. My child is with You and I am here on earth. I am setting my focus on the anticipation of meeting up with them in the future. Steady my heart. Sooth my ache of emptiness. Again, thank You for my child. Amen.

Day 64

2 Corinthians 1: 20 "For no matter how many promises God has made, they are 'Yes' in Christ. And so through him the 'Amen' is spoken by us to the glory of God."

WHEN I WAS at my lowest state in my grief journey God reminded me of what He said in His Word.

"You have turned for me my mourning into dancing; You have put off my sackcloth and clothed me with gladness, to the end that my glory may sing praise to You and not be silent. Oh Lord, my God, I will give thanks to You forever" (Psalm 30:11-12).

But Oh, my God, when? How? This pain is too much for me. I want relief now. I want to dance now and throw off my sackcloth now.

The promises of God are guaranteed but there is a time for them to be fulfilled—God's time. Throughout my journey I have watched God begin to work out this promise in my heart and life. Am I dancing yet? Getting closer. I have however; taken off my sackcloth and by faith I am giving Him thanks. I have witnessed and experienced my torn, broken, shattered heart beginning to heal and be restored. I am starting to sing praise to Him and not be silent.

How God does His work in us is a mystery and a miracle. We must ask Him and give Him a chance to prove His love and care for us. I believe one day I will be dancing and my deep mourning will be turned into morning—from darkness to the light of day! Believe this truth for yourself as you travel on this hard road of great loss—the light will break through.

Dear Father, I choose to put my trust in You. I choose to believe that You will bring healing to my shattered heart and that You will cause me to sing again. I lift up my heart, emotions and brokenness to You today. Bless me. Pour Your strength into me. Hold me steady. Give me a heart that relies on You more and more and a new song in my mouth. Amen.

Day 65

Isaiah 40:28 "Have you never heard? Have you never understood? The LORD is the everlasting God, the Creator of all the earth. He never grows weak or weary. No one can measure the depths of his understanding" (NLT).

IF YOU HAVE just begun your grief journey or have been on it for a while keep holding on to your faith and hope in the Someone bigger than your loss, bigger than your pain, bigger than your doubts and fears, bigger than your darkness.

The Bible says that God has searched each one of us and known us. He knows all about how we tick and how we are wired. He knows what we need in order to make it through these tough times. He created us with emotions and feelings. We love, we lose, we grieve, we grow.

No matter how bad your day is you will indeed make it through. Believe this. Press into that Someone who is big enough to give you the strength and grace you need for each moment—sometimes just to survive. Trust He is there.

The Bible says that the fool has said in his heart "there is no God." God has made Himself known to each of us in some way. We can see His handiwork in creation. His majesty and power. His tenderness and love. He has revealed Himself in the Bible. He created us to love just as His complete nature is love. Nothing happens by chance or bad luck or a fluke. Our God is so big He watches over His creation—His universe, His earth, His people, and the hearts of the broken and the needy—that's us. We are broken and needy.

God is big enough to meet your need even at this moment. Keep believing. Keep resting in the assurance of His love for you and His great compassion for what you are going through. Please do not lose sight of the larger picture. God has a plan and we are included in it as well as our child. Lean on the One who is Big and Strong and able to hold you up and bring you through. Trust Him with your precious child and begin to slowly move forward.

Dear Father, You made me just as I am. You see the tremendous pain in my heart. You see the bleeding and deep sorrow. Sometimes it is so hard to live and walk this journey. Sustain me. I believe You are big enough to carry me through this day. I place myself, my heart, my child, my ways in Your hands. Thank You for Your faithfulness. Amen.

Day 66

Psalm 36:7 "How priceless is your unfailing love, O God! People take refuge in the shadow of your wings."

O**UR CHILD IS** never really far away. We actually do carry their love—which never dies—within our very being. The Bible talks about love and says: "Three things will last forever—faith, hope, and love—and the greatest of these is love." (1 Corinthians 13:13) I did a little study on this and was very excited to find that the Greek word for "Forever" is *Meno*. *Meno* means to remain, abide, endure, continue, to be present. Love is a spiritual element and we are spiritual beings in a physical body. Somehow God allows the love of those who love us to remain within us. How? I think it is a mystery but I believe somehow our child's love for us is fused within our soul and spirit for all time. God is the God of love and His love is poured

out into our hearts
through His Holy Spirit.
God created love and He says it never dies.

Dear Father, let me become more aware of Your love in me and the love of my child. Thank You for the ability to love and be loved. I treasure and value my child's love for me. Love is stronger than death. I abide in Your love. *Amen.*

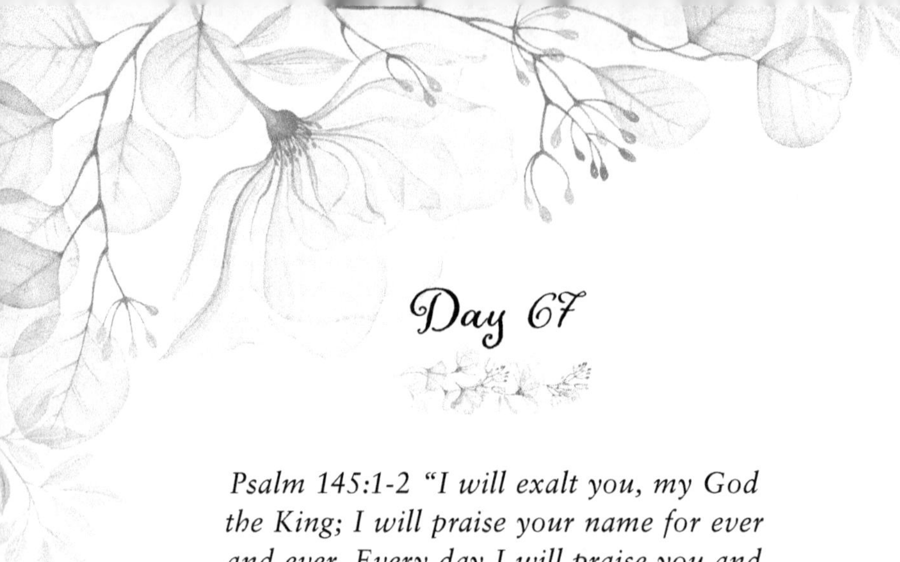

Day 67

Psalm 145:1-2 "I will exalt you, my God the King; I will praise your name for ever and ever. Every day I will praise you and extol your name forever and ever."

FOR THOSE WHO are finding it very difficult this Thanksgiving without your child this is for you.

Thanksgiving Prayer

Dear Father, this pain is deeper than I've ever experienced—my heart is broken. I don't feel happy or like celebrating anything—my baby is gone. I feel a loneliness steal over me. I feel a desperate hopelessness. Nothing seems to bring me comfort. All I know is that the joy of my life is not going to be at the Thanksgiving table with me.

Please Lord, help me to see what to be thankful for this holiday. My eyes are blinded by the grief I am swimming in. Open my eyes and show me Your comfort. Help me to get through each long sorrowing moment and to hold on to hope in You. I lean into Your love and strength. Support me and unblind my eyes to what You are doing in my life.

I lean into You, O Lord and praise You for You are good. You are wise and You will place my feet on solid ground. You will lift me up out of this miry pit and fill my mouth with praise and my heart with joy. I believe one day my sorrow will be turned into Joy and my mourning into dancing. How? I don't know but I trust that You will lead me there. **Amen.**

Day 68

Revelation 7:15 "Therefore, "they are before the throne of God and serve him day and night in his temple; and he who sits on the throne will shelter them with his presence."

I BELIEVE THAT EVERY time we celebrate Christmas here on earth they celebrate it in heaven. I can hear the angels singing and rejoicing celebrating the day that God sent His only Son, His Christ to earth to reconcile all mankind back to Himself. I can see our children and loved ones who have gone on dancing and singing, feasting and worshiping the Lord's Christ! The joy is unspeakable and the glory full and rich! Sorrow not for our child, for the Bible tells us there is no evil or pain in heaven just pure love and joy. If we listen close enough sometimes we can hear a great roar from heaven of saints and angels proclaiming lifting their voices adoring the memory of the baby King in the manger!

Let the peace of God wash over your wounded heart this

Christmas and holiday season. Let His comforting presence surround you. And as you lie down at night lean upon His promises and tender love for you. He is faithful.

Dear Father, let the beautiful wonder of Christmas fill my wounded heart. Let the Prince of Peace flood my heart with peace. Let the Joy of the Holy Spirit ignite my worn and weary heart. I rejoice with my son in heaven who is also celebrating the memory of Christmas. Amen.

Day 69

Isaiah 9:6 "For to us a child is born, to us a son is given, and the government will be on his shoulders. And he will be called Wonderful Counselor, Mighty God, Everlasting Father, Prince of Peace."

I BELIEVE OUR CHILD wants us to be living a full and contented life here on earth. I can imagine a Note from heaven to Mom.

Dear Mom, I am so very happy in my new home! I can hardly wait for you to be here and to see the beauty and awesome life we live here. We celebrate Christmas up here too! Christmas trees are beaming with lights and reindeer are actually flying all around! And yes Santa has a bag full of toys for the girls and boys. God loves to see us squeal with delight! Our Father is so good to us!

I am waiting for you Mom, and I want you to live your life with joy and purpose.

I am so sorry that
you are hurting. I want to
wrap my arms around you and kiss you and
tell you I am okay. In a blink of an eye we will be
together again!

I always love you,
Your only son,

Joseph David

Day 70

Proverbs 17:22 "A cheerful heart is good medicine, but a crushed spirit dries up the bones."

I'M THINKING ABOUT Christmas this year. It's different without my son. Last Christmas, the first year I lost him, was a huge blur and I did all I could to survive emotionally. This Christmas is so much better—my mind is clearer. I am going in and out of the past and the present. It was like that, but today it's like this. I am realizing daily that there are loved ones and friends who are here now and they feel my loss and they love me. I am determined to make some new memories and enjoy my life for this moment. Build stronger memories with my family and friends that have stood with me, and the new ones I am making. I want to embrace those alive around me and create loving memories that I will look back on in years to come. I want to make an impact in their lives and be a blessing to them.

You see I'm just a pilgrim passing

through this world on to the next where my permanent home lies. But as I am traveling through I want to live my life to the fullest and bring happiness wherever I go. Later when I'm in my new home in heaven I will get to replay all the memories I've made on earth. I believe, Joe my son, and I will sit down together and replay, even relive our fun memories together. We don't forget just because we are in a different location.

I know it is difficult but try to create at least three new memories this holiday with those who care about you.

Dear Father, during this holiday season please help me to focus on those around me. Even though there is pain in my heart, help me to choose to love and give out to others who need me. Give me the courage and strength to make some new and lasting memories. Show me what to do. Show me how to celebrate with those with me in my present. Amen.

Day 71

*Isaiah 9:6b "And he will be called
Wonderful Counselor, Mighty God,
Everlasting Father, Prince of Peace."*

WE WILL ALWAYS miss our loved ones who have left this life. We've made so many memories together—they have become part of us—such a deep part of our being.

I believe they will be celebrating with us this season just in another place—though not far way.

I so missed Joseph the other day and got caught up in my memories and thoughts of never seeing him again this side of heaven. Christmas began to feel painful to me. Then God infused hope into my soul. Somehow I began to see the Christmases past and how much fun they had been and that they would always be in my heart, but this season was a new season for me to embrace and to create new memories.

I will always remember yesterday with my beautiful child. However, now I look forward to seeing him in the future. He will be my precious gift when I get to heaven. But today—I choose to enjoy the season. To go to dinners and buy those gifts for loved ones. To dress up in my colorful scarves and boots and smile

at the world rejoicing that the Christ child
came to reconcile the world unto God.
I will make hot cocoa and kiss and
hug loved ones. Every day is special
and a gift to me. I stumble but get
up again. I choose joy in the midst
of sorrow.

Dear Father, Oh, widen my borders so I can give out to all who need your love this season. Help me to remember to make each moment count. That each hug and kiss and cup of hot cocoa is a sweet thing to my soul and not to discount even the smallest joy that comes into my life Amen.

Day 72

John 1:14 "The Word became flesh and made his dwelling among us. We have seen his glory, the glory of the one and only Son, who came from the Father, full of grace and truth."

IT IS NORMAL to feel afraid of remembering memories of our child—especially during the holidays. What are we afraid of? The pain and the ache that may accompany them.

As I was Christmas shopping I saw some children with eyes so wide with wonder and joy as they stared at all the holiday decorations in the mall. I thought, *oh that little boy looks like Joe did at that age.* I was afraid to remember. Afraid of feeling the deep pang of sadness again. But it happened. Memories of Christmases past flooded my mind and grabbed at my heart. I envisioned our home all decked out with decorations of red and green, shiny bulbs, the little village. We were celebrating the birth of Christ with great joy indeed! I had my little son with me and we danced about with Christmas songs playing.

The joy I felt at that moment quickly turned into sadness as I remembered that our son was no longer going to celebrate Christmas with us. More memories, more joy, more sadness—and then tears. Oh how I miss him so much.

Dear Father, please help all of us who have lost a child to find some joy during this season. Help us to find our joy in knowing that You came to our earth so we could know You personally and Your love for us through Your Son, Jesus. And please help us to allow ourselves to remember our precious memories of our child—all the years, all those holidays and to be so thankful we had them.

Again, please stitch up our broken bruised hearts so we can laugh again and bring joy to others. Strengthen us moment by moment as we walk this journey and remember. Amen.

Day 73

Psalm 91:4 "He will cover you with his feathers, and under his wings you will find refuge; his faithfulness will be your shield and rampart."

Christmas Prayer:

Dear Father, give me Your perspective this season. Please help me to keep centered as best I can. Show me glimpses of Your love and Your glory. Lead me to the people who can help me heal—to the places—the books, the circumstances. Open my eyes to Your Word and strengthen me by Your Holy Spirit. I don't care what others say about me I just know that I want to place my complete reliance on Your faithfulness. I pledge my allegiance to You and choose to stake my life on all You have said in Your Word.

Please give me some glimpses of joy this season—and laughter. I thank You for my child and the moments we shared together. Tell them I love them and can't wait till we meet again. Give them a hug and a kiss from me. Thank You again loving Father, I ask this in the name of Your son, Yeshuah the Christ. **Amen.**

Day 74

Luke 2:14 "Glory to God in the highest heaven, and on earth peace to those on whom his favor rests."

I HAVE THOUGHT OF different ways how we might survive the holidays without our child. I could see that if I continued to allow myself to be controlled by my emotions of grief I would go down that rabbit hole. I prayed. Prayer works.

I thought—how can I hold the perspective of juggling the expectant joy during this season and the stinging ache of remembering my child throughout past Christmases?

I'll tell you what shift in my thinking I began to cultivate. I began to find all the things that I could be thankful for. Who wants to be thankful when they're grieving? I chose to find all the good things in my life that I could be grateful for. For each of us we will find many reasons to thank God.

I thought of my husband, Ike, he is a good man and has helped me through the roughest parts of my grief journey. He knew how close Joe and I were. Then of course for my beloved child and our memories. And then I have my health—I can walk and I am not blind. I can see all the decorations and the lights aglow. My family I grew up with—they are such a strength to me. My refrigerator bursts of bountiful food. Our car has not caused us major problems that could eat up our money. My closet is filled with beautiful clothes …and so on.

What are all these things compared to my child? They can't ever be compared but it is a start in helping me change my mind set out from a heavy cloud of deep sadness to something I can manage.

I decided to begin to gather some new Christmas decorations —maybe one ornament to start with that portrays new hope and joy. Maybe I'll keep the old decorations in their boxes—it would be too painful to put them up—at least at this time. I want to start a new tradition but don't know what that is yet.

Then of course choosing to rejoice in the Messiah, Jesus Christ, who came into our broken darkened world to bring "forever hope" and good will towards men."He who made the way possible to be with our child forever throughout eternity" (Laura Diehl *Hope for the Future*).

I played Christmas carols in my car and decided to really think about the words I was hearing—I decided to allow my heart to be somewhat happy.

And you, dear Mom, you too will survive this holiday season without your child by putting one foot in front of the other and you will have grace and strength for each moment. When you feel overwhelmed with grief, pray. Prayer works and can bring us out into a new place.

Dear Father, please bring me into a new place in my mind and heart. Remind me of the blessings You have given to me and my family. Give me the strength and determination to cultivate a heart of gratitude and thanksgiving. Thank You for allowing me to be alive today. Thank You for the courage I need to continue on this journey. Amen.

Day 75

Deuteronomy 33:27 "The eternal God is your refuge, and his everlasting arms are under you" (NLT).

THE EVERLASTING ARMS

Where are God's arms? Underneath us to hold us up and to strengthen us on our journey of life. Not only does He hold us up but it is in His presence that we can find peace and security. Psalm 91:1 says that we can dwell in the shelter of the Most High and when we choose to dwell in the place where God is, rest is the result.

This busy season of hustle and bustle and strong emotions of joy and sadness—rejoicing and grieving, God asks us to take time out to gaze upon His beauty in His dwelling place and fellowship with Him. The result will be rest and peace of mind.

Dear Father, today I take this time to spend with You and to think upon Your goodness and beauty. I choose to hide my soul in the shelter of Your wings. Give me rest, O God, give my soul rest and peace. Calm my fears and hold my tears. *Amen.*

Day 76

A PRAYER FOR THE NEW YEAR

DEAR FATHER, HERE I am a mom who has experienced a great loss—my child. When I think of facing the New Year I am overwhelmed at what I will have to go through. More pain, more anguish, more aching for what will not be this side of heaven. I can't do this on my own. I need Your perspective on my loss. I need a strength and a comfort far beyond what I can contrive. I need Your strength and grace. Please pour it out on me right now.

I am limping into the New Year. Oh Father, I cry out to You to heal my broken heart—to mend it and make it whole. Help me to see the light at the other end of the tunnel. Take my hand and walk with me through this grief journey. Quiet the constant sorrow and comfort me with Your Word.

Dear Father, I believe that my child is safe with You. You will take care of them for me. Please open my heart to grow in my faith and to find You and *be aware of what You are doing in my daily life. Guide my footsteps to the people, places and things that will help bring about my healing.*

Dear Father I release myself and my grief into Your hands for this New Year. Let me walk a little lighter—to find my way a little easier. Help me to be comforted with the promise that because You live I shall live also and will join my child again. It is not goodbye—rather it is see you soon.

I love you Father. You are good. You have brought me through this last year and You will bring me through this new year—moment by moment—step by step, day by day, teaching me, guiding me, loving me, comforting me.

And so my Father, give me a heart after You and help me to be kind and compassionate to others and to help those You bring into my life who have also lost a child so I can encourage them on this difficult journey.

Praise You and thank You. These things I pray in the name of Your one and only Son, Jesus Christ, Messiah and Savior. *Amen.*

Day 77

Isaiah 28:10 "He tells us everything over and over— one line at a time, one line at a time, a little here, and a little there" (NLT).

I ALWAYS THINK IT is a good idea to make some time to get alone and reflect after holidays or when I've been around many people or been very busy.

Today I sat alone on my couch and I thought about my life. I thought about going into the New Year without my son. I miss his smile—oh I know you understand. I studied some of his photos—it seems like he's been gone for a long time and yet seems like only yesterday he was with us. February it will have been only two years since our loss of Joe.

I love what one wise mom said about each day we live. She said that instead of getting further and further away from our child we are actually getting closer and closer as our days go by. I know I am really anticipating that day when I see Joe again.

As I reflect on my life I see that I am not so much in a hurry to do things—to accomplish—to produce. I will do all these things naturally when I have the energy. I have placed my plans in God's hands. I rest in what He is doing in me at this season of my life. Little by little one step at a time is how we grow in our lives. We live moment by moment and gather wisdom a little here and there. We steadily build one layer upon another of hope, faith and love. Again sometimes we just "Be" that mom who again mourns her child. And then again that mom who dares to take shaky steps out onto the unknown path before her.

I am learning that to savor life we must be present in our moments and rest in the assurance of a love that is stronger than death.

Dear Father, when I feel overwhelmed pull me back into my present. Give me the ability to live in my now—balancing my past with my present and future. Work in me what only You can as I live and breathe each second of this day. Enable my heart to stay connected with the things You have planned for me to fulfill today. Thank You for loving and accepting me right where I am. Amen.

Day 78

I REALLY WANT YOU to know how much God, your Creator and Father in heaven, feels for your broken heart. Loved ones and friends leave us and that is the way of this life. Only one will remain the same and always be there for us—that's Jesus. In God's mercy He has a plan to bring you through this difficult season of grief. Draw near to His heart and ask Him how He wants to do this. Remember this is not the end of your child, there will be the reunion— God hates separation. Just be sure you are prepared

for this wonderful day that will be revealed in your future. Prepare by walking close with your God and His Son Jesus who made it possible for us to be with our child again.

Dear Father, please show me again how to heal. Where I need to go, what I need to do and who I need to see. Direct my paths. Thank You that I will see my child again in the future because I know You and Your Son, Jesus Christ. Help me to walk closer in step with You as I struggle through this journey. Amen.

Day 79

Psalm 90:12 "Teach us to realize the brevity of life, so that we may grow in wisdom" (NLT).

IT WAS JUST yesterday I could hear your voice—I could hear chuckles and laughter. As I looked at photos of you today I shook my head in a moment of disbelief—how can it be? You were just here now you are gone. You filled our home with such life and busyness. It is so quiet now.

We were planning to move into a new place—Dad, you and I. We were going to get a puppy—a golden Lab. It didn't happen. We were paralyzed with grief and stayed put until the time was right again.

What happened to all our time together? I'm studying the photos and somehow I can't put it all together to make good sense. You WERE here. I remember. It was just yesterday I brought hot dogs into your bedroom for dinner.

And then you called me to see something funny on television and we laughed together. But your room is filled with my artwork now and the empty bed unslept in. It was just yesterday when I hugged you and told you I loved you.

Day 80

Matthew 6:34 "Therefore do not worry about tomorrow, for tomorrow will worry about itself. Each day has enough trouble of its own."

IT HAPPENS AT night when my husband is asleep and I am awake. I begin to go over memories of my son. I process my grief—I think about it and him. Sometimes I cry and sometimes I don't. I always turn to the Lord and ask Him to show me how to live with the constant pain of missing my son. How to live a happy life apart from my son. I think one of the keys He has shown me is to live wholly in the present. When I begin to look at my future with dread instead of anticipation because I imagine myself with the companion of grief attached to my heart, it's more than I can bear. I cry out to God and He reminds me to come back into my present for there He will meet me and give me strength and comfort. I can stand anything for a few moments. God pours strength into my being—it is really a miracle how it happens but it happens over and over again. I can face my present and as I press into my present I can live life fully. Even experiencing pain and sorrow, joy and laughter is being alive. Enjoying those in my life that I love is being alive.

Dear Father, teach me how to live in my present and embrace all I go through so I can experience real living. Instruct my heart and mind how to come back into my present when I feel overwhelmed with pain. I will train my heart not to borrow from tomorrow—fears, worries and concerns. Thank You that I have all I need to make it through each moment of each day. Amen.

Day 81

Luke 4:18 "The Spirit of the Lord is upon me, because he has anointed me to preach the gospel to the poor; he has sent me to heal the brokenhearted, to preach deliverance to the captives, and recovering of sight to the blind, to set at liberty them that are bruised" (KJV2000).

YOU CAN'T HURRY grief. There is not a pill that will take away the pain and heal your broken heart. There is no fast—*get it over now*—formula. You have to go through it.

I remember in the beginning of my grief journey when it hurt so deeply I wanted it to go away right then—I wanted it to pass quickly. I tried to rush it but couldn't. It came right back. I kept riding the waves of grief and thought maybe this time I would stay on the shore but it drew me out again. I felt overwhelmed at the thought that I might have to struggle for a long time. I had to bring myself back to the moment where I had the strength to cope. I counted the days hoping that the passing time would make it go faster. But my days were up and down—like the waves ebb and flow. My emotions all over the place. I still felt lost, lonely, displaced and frightened. I was told again that I had to go through all these emotions processing and working through them. I would cry out to God to take away my pain and to heal me—heal me quickly.

As the first year passed and I entered into the second year I found it was true. We do heal—it does get better—it does ease if we face it and process through it with the help of others who have been through it—the help of those who have learned ways of coping and thinking about their grief in healthy ways. If we place our faith in God and trust His Word—if we reach out to help others—if we determine to grow we will heal.

God has brought much healing into my life gradually. At times I fall back into the missing and ache of loneliness for my child. But I know how to come back out of that frame of mind so that it no longer controls my life. God has been stitching up my broken torn heart and that takes time.

Please be patient and gentle with yourself—you've been through a lot. Learn about the process of how grief works and live moment by moment by God's grace.

Dear Father, keep taking me through this grief process. Give me courage and bravery to meet it daily. Take away the anxiety and fear I feel when I can't seem to go on another day. Make me brave. Give me eyes to see light ahead. Amen.

Day 82

*Psalm 48:14 "He is our God forever and ever,
and he will guide us until we die" (NLT).*

IN THE BEGINNING of my grief journey I used to fear that I would feel bad forever. It frightened me to think I would feel this anguish and deep pain for years and years. But it does get better if we daily face it and work through it. It gets better if we press into the Lord and get our hope and strength from Him. It will get better when we see it in the right perspective. It does get better when we reinvest our lives in helping others in their pain.

We will be given a choice at a crossroad in our grief journey whether we will keep moving forward into healing or stay in our dark hole.

Will we be rid of our pain and sadness? We will always remember but the pain will dull and the sadness lighten. Will we ache for them? Yes always, but we

will make it through
this valley with God as
our guide.

Day 83

I Peter 5:10 "And the God of all grace, who called you to his eternal glory in Christ, after you have suffered a little while, will himself restore you and make you strong, firm and steadfast."

WITH SUCH A traumatic loss of a child it takes much courage to face each day and work through our grief again and again. For those who are just beginning this journey I want you to know that you are courageous and you will make it through all this blinding pain and sorrow. For those who have been on this grief journey now for a while—I commend you for holding on to hope as best you can and giving yourself a chance to mend.

I have heard it said that your heart will never heal from losing your child, but I disagree. You will never forget them. You will miss them immensely as long as you live. But if you let it, your heart can heal. Some choose to stay in the shadows of grief because they may think if they feel better they are betraying their love for their child. No. No. To come full circle *through* your grief you show how much you love your child for you are brave. With the love of your child within you, you can heal. Your precious one would be very proud of your bravery and courage.

Will you feel the terrible sorrow and pain always? No. I don't believe you have to feel this forever. You will remember but the memories that once brought such grief won't hurt as much—your step will feel lighter. But oh, if it is your season to grieve— you must. Even in your grieving state you can be gently healing inside as you process your thoughts and feelings. And don't forget the One who created your heart and soul knows how to bring you healing. You have to want it and ask Him to show you the way. When you are ready—you will know it.

Day 84

Ecclesiastes 4:9-10 "Two people are better than one because [together] they have a good reward for their hard work. If one falls, the other can help his friend get up" (GOD'S WORD Translation).

TODAY WAS A teary day for me. I tried to figure out why. I came to the conclusion that it was the news I received about my brother being in the hospital. That made me sad and vulnerable to my feelings of grief. I began to miss Joe. I remembered things about my Joe. His first girlfriend, the way he would clown around with me, his sweet gentle spirit that kept me company so many times, and the cute little house we raised him up in, his playmates as a child. When I got home from being at the store I looked through photos and watched a birthday video we had made with him on his sixth birthday. Tears streamed down my face and my husband was also feeling weary and sad. I went into Joe's room and it smelled like him. I touched his shirts and wallet. I looked over at his bed and surely missed him with everything within me. Then after a while I decided I needed to switch my focus. So I started to work on a painting, and shared a muffin (yes, of course chocolate) and decaf coffee with my husband. We comforted ourselves. And I touched Joe's photo on the fridge and told him I would see him again—I just have to be patient and continue my work on earth.

I heard God whispering to my heart that He was there whenever I needed Him. He was my sure comforter and strength. He would always see me through.

And you dear mom, today may be a teary day for you—but you are not alone in this journey we are walking together. Remember feelings and moods change so don't be fooled into believing you will never feel good again. That's just not true. And what God whispered to my heart He is whispering to yours right this moment. "I am here for you and I will help you through this journey because I love you."

Dear Father, Oh how I miss my child with every breath I have. I know when my tears fall You gather them up and put them in a special bottle preserving them for something I know not of. My tears are very precious to You somehow. Today I lean into Your great love for me and I put all my trust in You. Amen.

Day 85

Romans 12:3 "For I say, through the grace given unto me, to every man that is among you, not to think of himself more highly than he ought to think; but to think soberly, according as God hath dealt to every man the measure of faith" (KJV).

As a grieving mom you will find yourself somewhat on what seems like a roller coaster ride. At least in the beginning stages. Our emotions are all over the map and frankly they should be—we just lost a gigantic part of ourselves—our sweet child. We are bleeding and broken and nothing makes sense. We feel we are in a nowhere land. Please try not to be alarmed or afraid very long—this is all normal on the journey of grief.

I think what really encouraged me in the beginning and helped me get a little better footing of what I could, was my faith in a God who loves and is good. The Bible tells us we don't have to understand everything but we can place our reliance on God who will see us through this agonizing journey. So use your faith. Everyone has a measure of faith they are given.

Also by being in grief groups that are encouraging and not just sad was a big helper. When choosing a group find one that you feel safe to share your feelings in and where you will learn some tools on how to manage and maneuver through your grief. *Grief Share* and *Umbrella Ministries* are two really good groups. Check for them in your area.

Please know you are not alone in all of this—others have gone and are going through this grief process. One day you may feel terrible and not want to face the day. Other days you may feel you have no strength or hope. And then other days you may feel you are making some progress. Then after a while one day you will wake up and know that you indeed really will make it through.

Dear Father, You said for me not to lean upon my own understanding but to wholly trust in You. I surely don't understand why my child had to die before me. I can't make sense out of it. But I choose to trust in You because You are good and You love me. I trust You to bring me through this day today. Thank You for the people You have brought into my life to help me on this difficult journey. Amen.

Day 86

Psalm 9:9-10 "The LORD is a shelter for the oppressed, a refuge in times of trouble. Those who know your name trust in you, for you, O LORD, do not abandon those who search for you" (NLT).

EVERY ONE OF us is in our own stage of the grief journey. For some we have learned to make the most of what we have and who we are with—the sorrow is not as overwhelming and consuming as in the beginning. Yes, we still grieve the missing presence of our child—we always will—they were such a connected part of us.

I want to address those of us who have recently lost a child and are at the beginning stages of grief—even those who may be past the first few years but still feel it so deeply that they are drawn back into that dark cloud.

To you dear mom: I can relate to how you are feeling. I know the pain is so deep you think you'll drown in your sorrow. But you won't— you will survive—moment by moment. I want to encourage you to press into the Lord. Press into His love for you even if you can't feel it right now—it's there. Take care of yourself and be kind and gentle to yourself. Be good to yourself. Do what you can do and let the rest go or perhaps you can get someone to help. This is a huge thing that has happened—Your child died. It affects every part of you. Your emotions, mind, soul, spirit, entire physical being. You are exhausted and cry easily. This is so very normal. You will get through. Surround yourself with good people who love you. Let yourself grieve—this is your time. But don't lose hope. Jesus said He would be there for you if you just call on Him.

Dear Father, pour hope into my fainting heart. Give me the assurance that You are with me during this painful season. Give me glimpses of confidence that I will indeed make it through these days—I will survive this storm. Help me to be gentle with my heart. I lift it up to You. Keep me, O God, keep me safe in You. Amen.

Day 87

WHEN I THINK of my child I think of love. I never knew that this kind of mother-child love was so intense, so pure and wonderful until it happened to me. I became a mother and my heart began to sing! I fell in love with this tiny being and wrapped myself around him.

God created mothers uniquely— able to keep pouring pure love into the heart of her child.

I found a Mother's Day card that Joe gave me. He would always forget the envelope when he chose it in the store. I loved him even for that. He was probably so excited to bring it home and write in it and give it to me. It didn't need an envelope—just love.

In the card he writes: *Hi Mom, I love you very much and I am happy*

I've been able to spend my time growing up with you. Happy Mother's Day, Joseph.

That is love. I love my son even though he is not with me—his love remains deeply entwined around my heart. A mother's love never ceases for her child.

Try to remember the little things your child did to show you they loved you. Hold them to your heart. Cherish them. Let them make you pause a minute and smile and feel warm and fuzzy inside.

Dear Father, thank You for blessing me with a child to love and who loved me. Thank You that the cords of love between us never break but remain and grow stronger as the days go by. Thank You that every Mother's Day I can remember the greatness and joy of being a mother. Please bless all the mothers in the world. Amen.

Day 88

Psalm 16:11 "You make known to me the path of life; you will fill me with joy in your presence, with eternal pleasures at your right hand."

I AM DETERMINED TO dance I am still learning the steps and the moves that are beautiful and graceful. I am determined to live a life of joy in remembrance of my son, Joseph. Instead of remaining in sadness and darkness—I will rise. I will tell the world how good God is and that He loves us so much. Where the enemy of our souls tried to shut me up and out through the death of my son—God, in His great power, has made me to stand! He will show me the

paths of life and joy as I walk with Him. What was meant to bring me evil will be turned into something that will bring blessing.

Don't let the enemy of your soul defeat you. Even in our darkest day the Light still shines and as we walk towards it we will rise.

Dear Father, keep my eyes focused on You and where You are calling me. Teach me how to keep on dancing in step with You. Place a determination deep within my soul to rise up out of the darkness of grief. Thank You that You are right now working out good for what was meant for evil in my life. Praise Your name! Amen.

Day 89

Genesis 1:25 "And God made the wild animals of the earth after its kind, and the tame animals after its kind, and everything that crawls on the ground after its kind. And God saw that it was good" (New Heart English Bible).

ONE OF THE most painful things I had to do was to give away Joe's dog, Furby. For short we called him Furbs. When we moved to Orange County we couldn't take him with us. It was like an end to that season of our lives with Furby as part of the family. As I said goodbye to Furbs I kissed him on the nose and cried. The dog and the boy. They just went together. They grew up together.

As I look back I have tears. I wish it all had been different. It was like that dog was a connection to Joe's childhood and early teen years. Furby was gone. And Joe's childhood gone. In his high school years we thought Orange County would be a better place for Joe to make good friends. It wasn't—we ended up moving back to the desert after four years. Trying to make new and happy memories and then Joe's life on earth was over—just like that.

I guess I mourn Joe's childhood and early teen years

where life was happier—Furby would pull Joe down the street on his skateboard. They would wrestle together. Joe's room was Furby's room. The dog and the boy.

I grieve what could have been and wasn't. I mourn the loss of my son once again. Slowly I pull myself up and write this blog for you moms. I know you have been there or are there now. We cannot stay in the past. We must look forward to the future where we will run into our child's arms again. But oh, we miss them don't we. I do believe this is the hardest part of grief—the empty spot where our child had been.

And, yes, I do believe our pets will be with us in heaven for God has designed all things in heaven for our joy.

Dear Father, comfort my heart in the remembering of my child's growing up years. The tender years. Comfort my longing heart. Satisfy me with Your presence and person. Take away my loneliness and give me grace not to stay in the past. Help me to keep my focus on the future where my child's life has continued. Amen.

Day 90

Hebrews 10:23 "Let us hold tightly without wavering to the hope we affirm, for God can be trusted to keep his promise" (NLT).

WHAT WILL YOUR mindset be today? How you think and what you are saying to yourself have a huge affect on how you handle your grief emotions. We are always talking to ourselves within our thoughts and much of the time we don't stop to see what we are saying. H. Norman Wright, Grief and Trauma Therapist, says that it is helpful if you write out a "Mourner's Creed." An "I Believe" Creed to say aloud to yourself every day. An example would be:

1. "I believe God's promises are true."

2. "I believe heaven is real."

3. "I believe I will see my child again."

4. "I believe God will see me through."

5. "I believe nothing can separate me from God's love."

6. "I believe God has work for me to do." (Wright, *Missing the Child You Love*).

What you tell yourself you will eventually really believe. If these are some truths you want to believe then make them your own.

God tells us in the Bible to think on things that are lovely, pure, and of good report. If your mindset is in a slump of gray thoughts, black thoughts, sad thoughts, fearful thoughts, begin to gradually add your own "Mourner's Creed" thoughts and it will help you to feel like you have some kind of an anchor to hold on to and are not just floundering away when your emotions and feelings are rising and falling like a tidal wave. "Believe you will have better days to come."

Dear Father, help me to be aware of what I am telling myself especially when I am feeling down or overwhelmed. Give me the strength to replace the dark thoughts with good and wholesome thoughts. I believe that better days will come. I believe that heaven is real and that I will see my child again. Amen.

Day 91

John 1:5 "The light shines in the darkness, and the darkness can never extinguish it" (NLT).

REMEMBER TODAY IT is one moment at a time—one step at a time. You can handle anything if you stay in the present moment. You have enough grace and strength to go through your day. Allow yourself to lovingly think of your beloved child and how much you love them. Think of a time they made you laugh! Do something special for yourself today and give someone a lift with a smile. Things do get better if you really want them to. Decide today that you will indeed make it through with God's help and not only will you make it through but you will come through victoriously and full of praise. Praise Him in the dark and you will begin to see the light.

God bless and watch over your broken heart today and gently continue the healing process. Much love to you.

Dear Father, I praise You in the dark times when the clouds hang over head. I praise You when it looks as if the pain will last forever. I praise You for Your provisions that You have given me to live through this day. I praise You for who You are! My God! My Rock! My Healer! My Deliverer! I love You Oh Lord, my strength. *Amen.*

Day 92

*Ecclesiates 12:7 "...and the dust returns
to the ground it came from, and the
spirit returns to God who gave it."*

WE DON'T KNOW why things happen the way they do. We don't know why our child was the one to leave this world and leave us behind. There are lots of questions. I know. We will never know or understand certain things this side of heaven—if God wanted us to know He would have told us. And sometimes He does. But to be stuck in the "why" mode will only take us in circles and bring frustration, anxiety and doubt.

Remember with me for a minute who GOD is. GOD is huge in understanding, wisdom, love, mercy. He sees all things, all hearts, everyone's past, present and future to come. There are things that God knew about our child that we didn't know. He knew the heart of our child and what his/her future held. Because God is always good and does all things out of a heart of love, I believe we can place our absolute trust in His reasons and ways with our beloved child. He created our baby. He placed breath and life into them. Our child first always belonged to God. He came from God's creative hand for us to love, nurture, teach and raise, and has gone back to his merciful Maker. Can we believe that it is well with our child? Yes.

Dear Father, I do believe it is well with my child. Because You live, he lives also. I know that You created my child's heart so You knew what made them tick. You knew them so well—better than I could ever know. You knew their secrets, their fears, dreams, hopes and desires. Thank You that You have received them unto Yourself to their home in heaven. Thank You for Your mercy and love to them. Amen.

Day 93

Psalm 136:1-5 "Give thanks to the Lord, for he is good. His love endures forever. Give thanks to the God of gods. His love endures forever. Give thanks to the Lord of lords: His love endures forever . To him who alone does great wonders, His love endures forever. Who by his understanding made the heavens, His love endures forever."

Dear Father in Heaven, please give me Your mindset concerning my child and this great loss. The emptiness I feel that will not be quieted. Let me see things through Your eyes. Give me spiritual vision. I choose to place my trust in You, Jesus. I choose You as my Savior and Lord. Please heal my broken heart—broken from a love that is so deep and that can no longer be held physically. Help me to turn my focus on to Your massive love for me and my child. Nothing will ever separate us from Your love.

Day 94

Psalm 139:17-18 "How precious are your thoughts about me, O God. They cannot be numbered! I can't even count them; they outnumber the grains of sand! And when I wake up, you are still with me" (NLT)!

YOU KNOW SOMETHING, our children are always with us in some way. I am finding myself throughout the day, just a brief moment here and there, remembering Joe's voice on a matter, what he would say, how he would react to different things. Sometimes I chuckle over it—other times my heart strings are pulled so much I am reminded of how much he is missed in my life. But in dreams, thoughts and memories, photos and videos of his music I have him with me. He cheers me on and I feel his undying love with me. Perhaps God allows us to keep our child alive by sometimes giving us glimpses that he/she is okay. By allowing us to feel their love or presence at certain moments.

God tells us He will never forget us—we are engraved on the palms of His hands. Maybe when He looks at His hands He sees the nail prints from the cross He died on that remained engraved after His resurrection and He sees us. He did it all for the love of us, His wandering children, to reconcile us back to Himself. He is always thinking about us as we always are thinking of our child.

It is a mystery—the relationship we have with our child that continues even after death. No, we can't hear their audible voice, nor can we see them or communicate with them as we used to when they were here. However we just have that sense that they are still alive and with us in some way even if we don't understand.

Day 95

Proverbs 16:24 "Pleasant words are a honeycomb: sweet to the taste and health to the body" (Holman Christian Standard Bible).

I'VE NOTICED THAT at times writing a letter to our child in heaven is an outlet to help heal and comfort us. We can keep a journal of letters to our child and imagine how they would answer us.

Letter to Joe in Heaven:

Dear Joe, my son, I've been thinking of you today. I went and got a Starbucks drink—remember how we loved those drinks together? Everywhere I am I miss you so very deeply. My world is not the same since you left. I've been keeping myself busy so I won't have to keep aching to see your smile and hear your laugh.

You are such a joker! Your jokes still make me smile and chuckle some. Your Daddy is missing you too. He sure thinks of you every day. We both talk of you often.

Now I can't wait to see all the things you have learned in

your new home! I am sure Jesus enjoys every minute with you. You were a joy for Him to create and bring into our world. What do you do every day? I know there is no earth time in heaven— there is so very much I don't know about where you are living. I know you are using all your gifts for God and have countless friends. Do they have skateboards in heaven? What does your mansion look like? I wish I could see you now, but I have so much to do down here. Assignments are appointed for me to do—more precious souls to help, heal and bring with me to heaven.

Joe, you are my son and will always be. You were a gift to us on earth and now you are a beautiful gift to Jesus and those in heaven. Remember I love you dearly—so dearly. Kisses and hugs to you.

YOUR MAMA

Dear Father, thank You that I can express my thoughts and feelings through words. Thank You for my imagination that can image all kinds of wonderful things concerning my child. I am glad that writing a letter to our child is another way we can bring healing into our lives. Amen.

Day 96

1 Corinthians 2:9 "However, as it is written: 'What no eye has seen, what no ear has heard, and what no human mind has conceived' — the things God has prepared for those who love him."

J OE'S LETTER TO me From Heaven as I Imagine: Dear Mom, I miss you and Dad so very much and every day I ask the Father when you are coming. He tells me not yet and that you have work to do for Him. Yes I remember everything we did on earth. You were the best mom a boy could ever have had!

Furby is with me just like you said he'd be. He never needs a bath and he can catch Frisbees really high. And yes, flying skateboards are all over the place—course I've got one. I picked out a red one for you to join me when you come.

Every day I go to school here to learn how to be a ruler in the Lord's kingdom. We are taught that we will rule and reign over peoples in the future. I study the Bible every day and the words come off the pages like light. They fill up my being. Mom, I am so very happy here. God is more than I ever imagined and Jesus, He is super! Holy Spirit dances around me every now and then and lifts me up into His arms. Grandma

is planting rose gardens and she is so funny. We laugh
so hard together! There is just so much life here and no
sadness, no evil or darkness. Oh Mom, I'm so happy
to be home! You should see me I have grown! And
Mom you don't have to worry about your weight up
here and you can eat and eat and eat! Got to go, the
disciples are having a bonfire and we are going to sing.
I'm leading the songs on a really super guitar! You can
watch the notes rise and fall in different colors.

Mom, remember I always love you and don't be sad
for me. When times get hard on earth for you just
know that I am cheering for you.

Love, Your Baby Boy, Joe

*Dear Father, thank You for my beloved child.
I praise You for heaven and its glory. Thank You for Your
presence and beauty that cover the entire heavens. Thank
You that there is joy in heaven! You are my joy. I choose to
rejoice in You today. Amen.*

Day 97

Isaiah 49:23b "Then you will know that I am the LORD; those who hope in me will not be disappointed."

"No one ever told me that grief felt so like fear" C.S. Lewis.

When I first found out the news of the death of Joseph my heart was filled with panic and fear. What would I do without him? How could I live without him? How would I handle my feelings and thoughts? My world was torn apart. I gasped.

Who would I lose next? My husband? A family member? My world was so unsure, so unstable. My

heart was overwhelmed. At times I would be terrified that Joe was gone and the house, his room empty. What would I do with myself? I took God's words literally that He would stick with me through this and see me through. That is just what He has been doing.

It takes many days for our shock of grief to lose some of its awful sting. But we are not left to ourselves. We've got the promise of our loving Father that He is with us. This means He hears our broken heart's cry. His presence surrounds us to comfort us. We are consoled by His Holy Spirit. Lean in on God—He'll never disappoint you.

Dear Father, when I remember the shock of receiving the news of the death of my child I hurt again—I feel horrified. Please soften that memory. Give me the eyes and heart to glimpse the reality of what happened. Gradually give me a heart to finally accept their death. Help me to forgive others who I may blame for their death. Father, hold me close today. Amen.

Day 98

2 Corinthians 10:5 "throwing down imaginations and every high thing that is exalted against the knowledge of God, and bringing every thought into captivity to the obedience of Christ..." (New Heart English Bible)

AFTER WE HAVE gone over and processed our thoughts about our child that were not pleasant, but rather painful, there comes a time when we must choose where to place our mindset. We must choose which thoughts to allow into our hearts which will in turn affect our emotions.

After struggling so many years with my son's bipolar and addictions I had a lot of painful memories along with the bright happy ones. The picture in my mind of my son suffering with tormenting thoughts and fears always brings emotional pain to me. I want to be kind to myself so I have decided to magnify the good and positive memories and to shrink the negative. The Bible tells us to think on what is good and lovely. It tells us to cast down imaginations that go against what God wants for us—He wants us to have peace instead of turmoil and torment.

I did, however, have to allow those painful memories

to surface in order to ponder upon them and find where I would file them away within my heart. I wept and hurt and mourned over them and then I felt it was enough so I placed them in the file that was put far back into the inactive files of my mind. So now if a picture of my son in suffering comes to me I thank God he is safe and healed and I guard my emotions by filing it away again. I switch to a beautiful thought of him instead. I want to cherish and meditate on the good times, the love, the warm memories. Admiring the special son I had with me for those years.

I accept what was but now those things are past. I am looking forward into the future with my son remembering the joy he brought to me.

Dear Father, when the heart wrenching thoughts and emotions come barging into my mind and heart show me how to process them. Help me to watch over my heart and to grieve the memories but then to place them away in the files of my mind. Give me the ability to focus and muse on the sweet and loving memories of my child. I lay the painful ones down at Your feet, Lord. Amen.

Day 99

*Psalm 54:4 "Surely God is my help; the
Lord is the one who sustains me."*

GRIEF IS OUR soul saying to our loved one, "I miss you. I love you. I want to be near you." Sorrow and Sadness is our soul saying, "It hurts to be apart from you. We've had precious times together." Tears are the voice of our soul without words but in a tangible substance validating how we feel inside.

Acceptance is our soul saying, "You are gone. I can't bring you back but I can fondly remember you and look forward to being with you again."

Faith is the substance that holds us together and brings healing to our soul, prodding us along.

God is the One who holds it all in His hand, understanding, comforting, restoring, mending, empowering and loving us.

> **Dear Father,** continue to give me insight into this thing called "grief." Help me to accept myself at each stage of this journey. Give me insight and wisdom on how to process my thoughts and feelings as I go through each wave of pain. Bring my heart to accept my lot and to believe that You will bring good out of it somehow. **Amen.**

Day 100

*Psalm 71:20 "Though you have made me
see troubles, many and bitter, you will
restore my life again; from the depths of
the earth you will again bring me up."*

OH HOW OUR Great Shepherd weeps with us for our lamb that is no longer with us. He holds our lamb close and sheds tears for our deep grief and sadness. Jesus says to us today as moms with broken hearts:

Jesus' Poem for a Broken Hearted Mom

"I was there, I was there when
   you're sweet baby died

And I carried her close as I
   stayed right by your side

I could feel all your pain
   and My own heart cried

Sweet Mama, Sweet Mama for
   your tears I died.

T'was hardest on Me when he drew
   his last breath

I knew what this meant to the Ones
   that he'd left

As I reached for his hand and drew him up near
I whispered I love you so much, in his ear.
As joy filled her being and happiness full
No sickness or pain she was free from it all
She plays now with angels and others like her
skipping and dancing without one single care.
But I don't ever forget as I bend down to behold
you, his dear mother carrying sorrows untold
Bent over in agony with a wound in your soul
That you feel just won't heal—the pain takes its toll.
I want you to know I've been here from the start
watching over your child and now over your heart
Draw up inside my blanket of love for you
And rest in each moment; I promise to bring you
    through.

Dear Father, thank You for Your promise to bring me through and to raise me up again from out of the pit. I am not destined to stay stuck in this dark dungeon forever, but rather destined to walk on the high places where there is victory with You. And even You will accomplish this in me as I lean into You daily. Amen.

www.ingramcontent.com/pod-product-compliance
Lightning Source LLC
Chambersburg PA
CBHW051448050726
47593CB00005B/1977